Living in the Power Zone

How Right Use of Power Can Transform Your Relationships

D1411997

Cedar Barstow, M.Ed.,C.H.T.

Reynold Ruslan Feldman,Ph.D.

LIVING IN THE POWER ZONE:
HOW RIGHT USE OF POWER
CAN TRANSFORM
YOUR RELATIONSHIPS

Copyright ©2013
Cedar Barstow and Reynold Feldman

All rights reserved.

Please contact the publisher for bulk orders of
"Living in the Power Zone."

First Edition, March 2013
Many Realms Publishing
Boulder, CO
www.rightuseofpower.com
info@rightuseofpower.com

ISBN#: 0-9743746-3-6

1 2 3 4 5 6 7 8 9 10

We dedicate this book to our parents
—Robbins, Meg, Jack, and Estelle—
who empowered us through their love and sacrifices
to both read books
and write them,
including this one.

With love and gratitude,
Cedar and Ren

When you eat a fruit, remember the people who
planted the tree.
(Vietnamese Proverb)

Acknowledgments

If it takes a whole village to raise a child, the same is true for producing a book. Ideas are like Lego pieces. They pre-exist any given construction and are simply reassembled by authors into something new. We therefore thank all those thinkers and doers, present and past, both friends and individuals known to us only through their writings, who have unwittingly collaborated in the creation of *Living in the Power Zone*. Saying they are too many to name isn't just a cliché; it's also a truth. So to all those individuals who have informed the thinking and writing of this book, we offer a sincere thank-you.

To those closer to home who have supported us in numerous ways, including through their unconditional love, we offer thanks as well: Our siblings and their spouses, as well as our children, step-children, grandchildren, godchildren, and "honorary" children. We also acknowledge our housemates, Doug McLean and Margaret Pevec, eye-witnesses to our periodic enthusiasms and funks, who always encouraged us and gave us that occasional knowing smile. You guys are the best!

Thanks to the members of Cedar's Women's Peace Circle—Sarah Hartzel, Judith Blackburn, Jean Lovell, Shelley Tanenbaum, and the late Linda Clark; Cedar's dear friends Amina Knowlan (who first came up with the concept of ethics as equivalent to the right use if power); Terry Keepers for his contributions to the section on shame; Charna Rosenholtz, and Anna Cox; colleagues in the Hakomi Institute; Ren's North Boulder-Sumac Men's Group; our beloved friends in Rungan Sari, Kalimantan, Indonesia, who helped us develop many new exercises and ideas for right use of power for everyone; our ministers and growing circle of friends at St. John's Episcopal Church–Boulder; the participants in Boulder's Spiritkeepers Interfaith Fellowship; and our brothers and sisters of Subud-Boulder, all of whom would ask about our work and be supportive.

Special thanks to our Advisory Team—Rich Ireland, Shelley Tanenbaum, Jenny Morawska, and Eva Fajardo; the Board of Directors of the new nonprofit Right Use of Power Institute (RUPI), Boulder—the Rev.

Dr. Marni Harmony, Chair—as well as the members of the Guild of Facilitators, Amanda Mahan, Manager. It's important to mention at this point that Marni was the individual who gave Cedar the idea for the 150% Principle, discussed later in this book. We are also grateful to the various Right Use of Power trainees whose words and impressions we have cited at various places in the text. They help justify the saying that teachers frequently learn more from their students than their students learn from them.

Special thanks to our graphic-design consultant, Marilyn Hager Adleman, for her elegant work as well as our contacts at Lightning Source Printers.

In conclusion, we would like to thank the God of our understanding, the Great Life Force, that has enabled us to be here, learn from our experiences, and assemble in this book concepts and tools which we hope will prove useful to you, our readers. Please forgive us for any mistakes or shortcomings, or better, send us your suggestions for improvement to **cedar@rightuseofpower or ren@rightuseofpower**. One of the benefits of print-on-demand books is that writers can easily revise and improve their works from time to time, and it is our intention to use your corrections and suggestions to do just that. So thanks in advance for your input.

Sincerely,
CD & RRF
Boulder, Colorado – March 2013

Table of Contents

Preface

Once upon a time there were two leaders, a kindly one and a mean one. The mean one was privately tutored by a scholar who loved the Renaissance ideas of Niccolò Machiavelli. According to this tutor, there were three things every sensible leader should do—gain power, increase power, and maintain the personal benefits achieved by power. The kindly leader, meantime, was privately tutored by a scholar who loved the ideas of Desiderius Erasmus, a Dutch contemporary of the Italian Machiavelli. According to this tutor, there was only one thing every sensible leader should do—use power for the benefit and well-being of his followers.

In the democratizing world of the 21st Century, it is no longer enough to have ethical leaders concerned with the common good. There are too few of them in any case. As important, possibly more so, is that we everyday citizens learn to use whatever power we have—and we all have some—in ways that increasingly benefit ourselves, others, and the world beyond. Numbers matter. So the more of us who learn to use our power well, the better the chances that our great-grandchildren and theirs will inherit a livable world where love trumps hate and peace has begun to vanquish war.

This is a brief, practical book. In eight short chapters we'll show you how you can use your personal, professional, status, and collective power with greater sensitivity and skill. In the Conclusion we'll summarize this material by listing out the *Power Concepts* and *Power Tools* you'll need to live a better, happier, more meaningful life and to help those around you do the same.

In addition, at the Right Use of Power Institute website (www.rightuseofpower.com) there are lots of free supplementary materials on using your power well. For example, you'll find tips and strategies for working with difficult people, be they bosses, co-workers, or subordinates; parents or children; teachers or students; customers or clients; spouses, partners, or even yourself.

A few words about us. Cedar Barstow, a certified Hakomi holistic psychotherapist and trainer, originally developed an ethics program back in the 1980s for the Hakomi Institute. As she began teaching this program, requests came in from non-Hakomi therapists to attend her workshops as well. Eventually in 2005 she published a long, somewhat technical book, *Right Use of Power: The Heart of Ethics,* to supplement her teaching. Its intended audience was helping professionals. Soon, however, people from outside the helping professions heard about her work and started coming to the workshops as well.

Up to now (winter 2013) Cedar has personally trained hundreds of people, from medical professionals in the United States to bankers in Australia to teachers in Indonesia to businessmen—and they *were* all men!—in Japan. She has also prepared over two hundred Right Use of Power facilitators, some of whom are now giving workshops of their own. It has meanwhile become clear to her that training in the wise, skillful use of power should not be restricted to helping professionals. This is a skill set we all need to have and use.

The world runs on power. Not just gas or electric power, but personal, professional, status, and collective power. (We'll define these terms in the Chapter One.) Yet as we are all aware, the long-term misuse and abuse of power in relationships large and small has put the future of our children and grandchildren, not to mention the planet itself, at risk. As a result, Cedar and some associates have founded the nonprofit Right Use of Power Institute in Boulder, Colorado. This institute envisions a world where a critical mass of humankind has learned to use their power effectively and well. The Institute's mission is to disseminate a range of products and services, including the present book, to help this dream come true.

The other author of *Living in the Power* Zone is Reynold Ruslan Feldman. A retired university English professor, dean, and part-time foundation official, he also happens to be Cedar's husband. As a multi-published author and editor who is himself a trained Right Use of Power facilitator, he was honored to be asked to co-write this book with Cedar. Since three of his books deal with wisdom for daily living, it seemed a small step for him to join with Cedar on a book project dedicated to helping others use their power wisely and well.

Let us be clear, finally, about our intent. It is, in a term made popular by bestselling author Malcolm Gladwell, to tip the concept into the world's consciousness that there are better and worse ways of using our personal, professional, status, and collective power. We look forward to the day when cars around the world will bear bumperstickers along the lines of "Got Power? Using it well?" We also hope that one day learning how to use power well will be part of the basic curriculum of every school in the world, beginning in pre-school.

Meantime, this book is intended as part of the effort to get the word out. Having a kindly leader here and there is no longer adequate (if it ever was) to assure a peaceful, harmonious world. In an age increasingly characterized by democracy, each of us must learn to use our power better for the greatest good of all. That's the proposition on which this book is based and to which it's dedicated.

We hope what we are about to share will prove helpful to you. For the truth is, each of us can choose the kind of leader we'd like to be. In this spirit, we wish you a good, productive read.

May you learn everything you need to know for living your life in the Power Zone.

The greatest revolutions science has presented to us across history point to others yet more fundamental waiting in the wings, hinged to a revolution of human spirit and ethic equally profound.

Joseph P. Firmage

My life belongs to the whole community; as long as I live it is my privilege to do for it whatever I can. I want to be thoroughly used up when I die. . . . When you make somebody else do something against their will, that, to me, is not power. That is force. To me, force is a negation of power. . . . By power I mean—almost exclusively—the ability to empower.

George Bernard Shaw

When the generativity and responsiveness of our power is guided by loving concern for the well-being of all, we will have an ethical and sustainable world. Power directed by heart. Heart infused with power. This is the key to right use of power.

CB

Power at its best is love implementing the demands of justice, and   justice at its best is power correcting everything that stands against love.

Martin Luther King

Introduction

"Hey, we have a new book. It's about power!" "Why would I be interested in that? I don't have any power," or "I already have it!" Either way, this book is for you.

We all have power and influence. Think of the power a baby has for getting love and attention. The definition of power is "the ability to have an effect or to have influence." In that sense, power is our birthright. Some of us misuse it, some of us disown it. Few of us get taught how to use it wisely and well. This book is your guide to owning the power you already have and then mastering your use of it.

Living in the Power Zone should have a major impact on your life. You'll learn that having power and influence is a given. As Harriet Ward Beecher said, "Greatness lies not in being strong, but in the right use of strength." You'll find out whether you tend to over-use or under-use your power. You'll come to understand the responsibilities, dynamics, risks, and strategies that accompany power roles whether you are up-power, down-power, or powerful because of your status in society or your membership in a group. You'll discover stories you tell yourself that both enhance and detract from your use of power. You'll deepen and expand your ideas about power, feedback, ethics, conflict, and shame. You'll increase your ability to feel empowered in all realms of life and know how to use your power with heart. In short, you'll learn how to live in what we call the Power Zone.

The eight chapters that follow prior to the Conclusion shed light on eight dimensions of using power wisely and well. Each chapter includes stories, strategies, and invitations to reflection. The "Try This" section has individual and group activities that will allow you to try out various Power Concepts and Tools. By learning about and developing more effective responses you'll improve your quality of life, both personal and professional. Observing, refining, and understanding your impact on others is a life-long engagement because using power well is an art, and like any other art, it requires daily practice.

Why did we write this book?

People frequently find themselves in situations in which they feel disempowered. Many have been deeply wounded by misuse or abuse of power from those in positions of authority. When a critical mass of people come to understand the nature and dynamics of power and how to use it with awareness, compassion, and skill, the world will become a better place. We want to de-mystify the concept of power, focus on it as relational, and help you come to understand it as *ethics in action*.

What do people want to know about power?

When Cedar's clients are asked what they want to know about power, they most often answer along these lines: *How do I heal from abuses of power in the past? How can I protect myself from future abuses? How can I re-empower myself? How can I deal with power plays? How can I get my therapist, teacher, or doctor to treat me with more respect? How can I best deal with a boss who doesn't treat me or my co-workers well?*

Here are selected reactions from participants in some of Cedar's Right Use of Power workshops:

Power is a feedback loop for self-knowledge.

I never knew that under-use of power was a misuse of power.

The adage "Do no harm" is inadequate for the best uses of power, which include repairing past harm and promoting well-being.

I can misuse power against myself by too much self-criticism and bad self-care.

I need to allow myself to make mistakes before I can allow others to.

I never knew how disempowering and prevalent shame is.

When I got in touch with my past wounding, I discovered that I had developed a lot of sensitivity around the issue, and there is a gift there that I can now use. I'm ready to claim my history differently.

I need to stand up for myself and get back up when I lose it.

I'm glad to know that there are four different power styles, not just the charismatic one that can cause so much bullying and harm.

It is not hierarchy that is the problem; it is <u>abuse</u> of the power role that causes harm.

I'm now confident that I can use my power with love.

I'm so relieved to be able to distinguish between my personal power and the professional power that I add on and can take off when I leave my job.

Power felt like the ability to take responsibility, make decisions, take action, and make a difference. Upon deeper reflection, I could feel a sense of "not for me." There was a fear of being accountable, not knowing what to do, doing the wrong thing, wasting power, being ineffective, and possibly making enemies. My thoughts about power were more absolute or dualistic, rather than a continuum. To my surprise, all this has now changed. [Leela Robinson]

We expect that after you finish this book, you will have similar reactions.

Learning to use your power wisely and well will equip you for life in challenging times. *Living in the Power Zone* will guide you in a practical and, we hope, enjoyable way to use your power wisely for the good of both yourself and everyone else.

Definitions

In the Right Use of Power approach, we honor and acknowledge our innate goodness and desire to serve. Here are a few working definitions

Power—Most simply it is the ability to act or to have an effect. It is what enables us to do things. *Influence* is how we interact with others to make changes and have an effect. *Role Power* is the increased power that accompanies a professional role. This state is called the *power differential*. *Personal power* is the generative capacity to use our gifts and make real our intentions.

Power With Heart—The use of personal, role, status, and collective power in which power as strength and power as compassion are blended and balanced.

Compassion—Resonating concern, an ability to see and respond to the connection between and among everyone and everything.

The Right Use of Power—The use of personal, role, status, and collective power to prevent, reduce, and repair harm; evolve relationships and situations; and promote well-being and the common good. *(In this context it is understood that power itself is neutral. It can be used in ways that foster harm or well-being depending on one's consciousness, skill, and intention. The use of the word* right *is not meant to imply a black-and-white concept of right vs. wrong or good vs. evil.)*

The Power Zone—The use of power with heart across a healthy range of appropriate responses in relationships and situations.

The Power Spiral—A visual model for practicing right use of power in the complex, swirling continuum of life.

Ethics—One dictionary entry defines ethics as the study of what is right and wrong and of duty and moral obligation. For our purposes, ethics is a set of values, attitudes, and skills intended to have benevolent effects on both ourselves and others when applied consistently in daily life. Other terms for ethical behavior are living in the Power Zone and using Power with Heart.

Chapter 1:

Owning Your Power and Influence

RIGHT USE OF POWER

CHAPTER 1:

Owning Your Power and Influence

"What do you know about power? What do you not know about power?" These are the questions we ask people in our workshops. Take a minute to notice what your responses are? Now here are some of the reflections we've heard in response to the first question: *"We've been taught that power is limited, but it really is unlimited." "Potential doesn't exist without power." "Power is not talked about. It's like it's the last of the four-letter words." "Power is seductive." "I have found ways to justify misusing power."* And here's what our workshop participants say they don't know about power: *"Why people refuse to see, won't or can't see how their power affects others." "Why I'm often not aware of using it." "What the limits of it are." "How other people experience it." "How I can have power that I don't feel." "When to stand firm and when to let go." "The relationship between justice and mercy in regard to power." "That place where vulnerability and power connect."*

The exploration of power and power dynamics is a rich territory. As a student of ours once said, *"We are somehow expected to know how to use power even though we are never taught about it."* An introvert as a child and young adult, Cedar thought the best way to help people and not hurt them was to avoid power altogether. She had no idea that to underuse her power was also to misuse it. Likewise, some of her more outgoing friends seemed unaware that their use of power could negatively affect others.

So let's start with the basics, some of which you may already know while others may surprise you.

Power is the ability to have an effect.

The actual definition of power is "the ability to have an effect or to have influence." For many of us, the concept of power, by contrast, has been experienced as manipulation, abuse, greed, violence, or intolerance and thus as a human capacity to be avoided. Likewise, it may have been associated with success, fame, fortune, control over others, and great influence and thus, for others, as something to be acquired, maintained, and increased. Because the actual definition is neutral, however, we get to choose whether to use our power in helpful or harmful ways.

Power is relational.

Since power is the ability to have an effect or to have influence, it is relational. There have to be others whom we affect or influence. Of course we can and do have effects on objects and processes as well. An example is the changes, mainly negative, we are now causing to our global environment. However, here we will focus primarily on our effect on other people. Understanding and working with the impact of our power on others is truly a lifelong undertaking. We need to learn how to increase our good impacts while diminishing the negative ones.

Own the power you have.

Power, or the ability to have an effect, is a birthright. Babies, for example, know without being taught to use the power of their tears and smiles to get the attention required for their survival. We need to own our power as adults to develop ourselves fully so that we can both survive and contribute to the greater good. We disown our power at our peril. As a client of Cedar's once said, "*Why are you talking to me about power? I don't have any.*" This book can thus be considered an "owner's guide" because we need to acknowledge and own the power we have, like it or not, before we can learn to use it well.

Ethics is using our power wisely and well.

Our definition of the right use of power is any use that prevents or repairs harm, improves relationships and situations, and promotes well-being and the common good. In other words, using our power correctly equals ethical wisdom and behavior. There have always been strategies for using power that are driven by ego, greed, and/or the need for control and fame. Consider the egregious abuses of power that white settlers of the United States perpetrated on blacks and Native Americans. In these instances, human casualties were considered the necessary and justifiable costs of the drive to conquer a *new* continent. Yet there are also approaches in which negotiation and peace-making are driven by a concern for the common good. In the long run, the latter uses of power will prove stronger and more sustainable than fear and violence. To summarize:

The ethical use of power and influence in human interaction consists of . . .

• preventing, resolving, and repairing harm.

• improving relationships and situations.

• balancing strength with heart.*

• promoting well-being and serving the common good.

Reynold Ruslan and one of our Hispanic Right Use of Power facilitators, Juan Felix Prieto of Dallas, Texas, came up with a good Spanish term for this balance: fuerazon, the combination of fuerza (force, power) with corazon (heart). Unfortunately, there is no similar possibility in English.

Balance your power with heart.

In the dominant paradigm in Western culture, where power is aligned with domination systems, it is assumed that one must choose between strength and compassion. Indeed, choosing one or the other *is* simpler. However, the greatest ally to using power with skill and wisdom is the ability to bring power as strength together with power as compassion.

In the words of a song by Charley Thweatt, it's all about "*standing in your power while staying in your heart.*" We owe it to both ourselves and others to learn and model this new, more neighborly paradigm. We understand heart to refer to a compassionate and resonating concern for all life that enables one to consider the needs of others as well as oneself and thus to treat others with respect, dignity, and kindness. Power aligned with heart creates ethics from the inside rather than the rule side in. In short, <u>power with heart is the ultimate art</u>.

Learning to use power well is not a linear process.

Learning to use our power and influence well is, to be honest, challenging. Yet we can learn from our mistakes. As Barry LePatner says, *Good judgment comes from experience, [and] experience comes from bad judgment.* Put differently, we learn in a spiral fashion. We believe there are Four Imperatives for using our power well: (1) Be Informed, (2) Be Compassionate, (3) Be Connected, and (4) Be Skillful. We build mastery little by little by refining our awareness, accountability, and wisdom. And yes, we will likely make mistakes along the way. But as the saying goes, growing older is required; growing up is optional. What's important is to learn from our mistakes. At the end of this book we describe a number of practices you might want to try as you work to become a masterful user of your power.

Right use of power requires more than good intentions.

"I'm not concerned about power. I've got all I need—good intentions." This is a common yet dangerous misunderstanding that can unintentionally cause harm. The road to Hell is famously paved with good intentions. Power, as we said, is relational. Relationships are complex. There are many reasons that our impacts may differ from our intentions. Cultural differences with others may cause our actions to be misinterpreted. Shame may impair our ability to relate in an effective way, or others may transfer feelings meant for someone else onto us. It's simply not possible, try as we may, to fulfill the Hippocratic Oath in our daily lives and *never* cause harm. But we *can* learn to track for any unintended consequences and then repair the damage as quickly as possible.

The Power Zone

The Power Zone is the name we have given to having a variety of responses within a healthy range that are appropriate to various situations and relationships. Staying in the Power Zone does not mean finding the center point and keeping balanced there, but rather being able to shift appropriately like an Aikido master who can swiftly and flexibly shift, turn, and handle whatever comes his or her way.

Four Kinds of Power

There are four kinds of power that we want to talk about in this book:

Personal Power

Personal Power refers to our individual capacity to have an effect or influence. As mentioned above, this type of power is something we all have by virtue of being alive. Although power is value-neutral, we do many things with it that make its use positive or negative. On one end of the spectrum, we diminish it, deny it, lose it, give it away, and forget it, while on the other, we over-identify with it, misuse or abuse it, increase it, fight for it, and frequently become addicted to it. By owning our power and exercising it in the healthy zone between the two extremes, that is, the Power Zone, we can use it magnificently, as one of Cedar's students once said. We can employ it with skill and sensitivity to prevent or repair harm and to promote the greater good. We can be powerful and compassionate at the same time. This kind of personal power is one of the most important things we hope you'll learn from this book.

Control, oppression, force, manipulation, and exploitation are the most common qualities associated with power of the Machiavellian variety. However, more effective in the long run are such qualities as kindness, the ability to collaborate, openness, enthusiasm, persuasiveness, thoughtfulness, self-awareness, sensitivity, non-defensiveness, honesty, and generosity. These characteristics are often found in individuals skilled in negotiating, listening, communicating, peace-making, and ethical decision-making. Knowing that we have choices in how to use our power is a potent gift, one in fact that is empowering.

We can also use or misuse our power toward ourselves through excessive and unnecessary criticism or self-hatred. But we can also notice when we've made a mistake and, with pride, make repairs and correct ourselves. We can disregard or disrespect our dreams and gifts and fail to become the person we could be, or we can use our power in the creative process of making our intentions real, manifesting our gifts, and embodying our aspirations. We always have that choice.

Story: *Henry, the client of a psychotherapist named Robert, complained of tightness and pain in his lower back and thighs. He also spoke of being constantly on guard for danger so that he could quickly* *take protective action. Robert asked Henry to show him how he guarded himself. Henry described having power in his fingertips that could send out flashes of lightning if anyone seemed threatening. As he said that, his whole body seemed to go taut. Robert asked Henry what his alertness was protecting him from. Henry replied, "My heart." Robert then requested that Henry take his awareness from his fingers to his heart and belly and notice what he experienced. After a long silence, Henry spoke. "I see that when I bring my power and awareness back to my belly, I feel strong and safe. But when I have my power out in my fingertips, I scare people and isolate myself. And, to my surprise, I feel desperate and much <u>less</u> powerful then. I'm being kind of a bully, but you know, I'm really more bark than bite." After another silence, Henry noticed that his lower back was relaxing. The pain was clearly connected with his putting his power outside rather than inside himself. Henry was over-using his power to protect himself, but as a result he became a bully.*

Role Power

Role Power, also called Positional Power or Assigned Power, is the increased power, influence, and responsibility that automatically accompany any assigned role. This power is acquired by being employed (by self or other), elected, or raised up above others. Some assigned-role examples are teachers, governors, doctors, priests, social workers, supervisors, executives, parents, business owners, and police officers.

Role power is an add-on to personal power—separate but connected. Nurses and policemen, for example, wear uniforms when they are at work in their assigned power roles. The uniform serves as a non-verbal sign that the person has an extra layer of responsibility and power. Often these individuals have special education or experience that prepares them for their responsibilities. Misunderstandings and/or grave abuses of power can happen when we over-identify with our roles. Think of dictators and abusive rulers throughout history who acted on the belief that their positions elevated them to the status of demi-gods who could do whatever they wanted with impunity.

Story: *Cedar's best friend's husband is a retired senior airline captain. When he was still working, he had a uniform, of course, and would typically be gone for four or five days at a time. His wife would manage their small farm, children, and household by herself while he was away. They experienced quite a bit of friction whenever he returned because he continued to act like an airplane pilot by taking charge and commanding everyone around. After the family sorted out the difference between his personal and role power, they came up with a ritual. Whenever he arrived home, he would take off his pilot's cap, hang it on a hook, and announce, "I'm home. I'm not a pilot anymore—I'm a partner and a papa." Things worked much better for the family from then on.*

Story: *Being able to put on and take off role power is helpful and important. I, Cedar, am grateful for my therapist's chair. It works for me like a uniform-substitute. When I sit down, I automatically move into therapist mode. I shift my personal life and issues to the background and focus on my client. My therapeutic empathy, knowledge, and skills come to the fore. My clients depend on my being in my professional role when I am with them. When I leave the chair, however, I am grateful that I don't have to carry my clients' sorrows and pains with me. I can leave my role—and their concerns—in the chair.*

We'll devote the next chapter to the relational dynamics that are set into motion when someone takes a specific role.

Status Power

Status Power is related to positional power but with a difference. Status power is determined and conferred by our culture. What do we mean by that? Okay, think of the respect with which older people are traditionally held, even today, in Asian society. Yet in Western and especially American society, being older doesn't automatically confer an aura of respect or authority. Quite the contrary. "There's no fool like an old fool," we say. And the growing incidence of senile dementia and Alzheimer's disease as we live longer seems to back that sentiment up. Instead of old people, we tend instead to romanticize youth.

With the status of our women, the situation is reversed. Feminism seems to have improved the position of women in the West, whereas in Asia and the Middle East they are still generally considered second-class human beings. Even though the official position of the People's Republic of China is that women "hold up half the sky" and are the equals of men, we recently had a 21-year-old female housemate from a city near Beijing. She told us that soon after she was born, her father left to marry another woman and thus have another chance for a son because his one child (China limits each couple to only one.) turned out to be a girl.

Traditionally, Chinese families preferred boys since they were physically stronger and considered more able to carry on the agricultural work that most families were then engaged in.

Here are some other examples. In traditional Hindu society, the priestly Brahman caste outranked all the others, including kings, queens, and aristocrats; merchants; and laborers. In Japan the most respected profession is still teaching. As a result, individuals with high positional power like prime ministers and members of the Diet (Parliament) are customarily addressed as *sensei*, teacher. How a public-school teacher in the United States would love to be accorded that kind of social esteem! By contrast we hear the expression in America, "Those who can, do; those who can't, teach." Or a final example: in Southeast Asian culture, physical labor and making money are considered less refined than studying spiritual texts or talking philosophy. Therefore in countries like Indonesia and Thailand, one will often see men with very long fingernails, especially on their pinkies. These indicate that they do not engage in manual labor. As a result, agricultural work and commercial enterprise are typically left to the women. Hence some of the richest people in those non-feminist countries turn out, surprisingly, to be female.

Status power also varies in terms of up- and down-power positions as perceived by individuals in different cultures. Think where you would place someone in your society based on such status measures as education, gender, sexual orientation, wealth, religion, or race. Cultural messages about power, often unconscious and unexamined, continually influence our beliefs about it, our responses to it, and how we use it. To use power sensitively, we must all take care not to be influenced by rankism: prejudice based on our perception of where others stand in society in relationship to ourselves.* For if we are unconsciously guided by such beliefs, we may mistreat some people or allow ourselves to be mistreated by others.

Having a uniform or its equivalent, like Cedar's therapist's chair, can help us transition in and out of our roles; however, in our daily lives we often move from role to role without noticing the shift. Lack of uniforms or changes of location add confusion. Status power in some cases is quite obvious but in others rather subtle, and as described above, it is generally related to a person's culture.

Just as an example, here's a chart showing some of the multiplicity of up- and down-power positions Cedar inhabits. *There is a blank copy of this chart in the Appendix that you can use to fill out for yourself. Note that several items can be both up-power and down-power depending on the circumstances. Also note that if Cedar were from another culture, some of her up-power status positions would be reversed.*

*For a fuller discussion of rankism, see Robert W. Fuller, *Somebodies and Nobodies: Overcoming the Abuse of Rank*. Gabriola Island, British Columbia, Canada: New Society Publishers, 2003.

UP-POWER: STATUS	UP-POWER: ROLE
Grandmother	Teacher
Woman	Therapist
Elder	Executive Director
White Person	Ethics Committee Member
Member of the Middle-class	Author
Graduate-degree Holder	Consultant
Home-owner	
A Healthy Person	
DOWN-POWER: STATUS	DOWN-POWER: ROLE
Woman	Patient in a Doctor's Office
Middle-class	Parishioner in a Church
(not in the One Percent)	Buyer Complaining to a
Senior	Corporation
Introvert	Passenger on an Airplane

In daily life we weave back and forth between and among these kinds of power many times each day, often without being aware of the shift. One's ability to have an effect or to have influence depends on a dynamic and mindful integration of personal, role, and status power.

PERSONAL POWER (a given affected by choice and circumstance)	given	role-based	ROLE POWER (a role-based add-on)
STATUS POWER (a given with some choice)	given		

Collective Power

The Japanese say, "One stick is easily broken, while ten bound together are not." Whether a single boy bullied by a gang at school (a bad use of collective power) or community members protesting against a harmful new ordinance in their town (a good use), there is power as well as safety in numbers. Teams can often solve problems better than an individual because of their pooled knowledge and wisdom. As a result, companies have come in recent years to depend on work teams to get significant projects done. That's how the lauded Boeing 777 jetliner got built. And as every fan of Western films knows, even the toughest sheriff raises a posse before riding out into the hills to capture the bad guys.

These days, using computer and internet technologies, one person can garner thousands of signatures on a petition for a political or social cause they believe in. Non-governmental organizations (NGOs) over time have used their collective power to effect many changes. So have labor unions. Gandhi and then Martin Luther King inspired and activated the process of non-violent resistance. We have heard many stories of people who on their own had little success in changing dysfunctional office policies. But when they got together with others, their collective leverage did the trick.

Story: *Several years ago our retired friend Judith saw a documentary and became so concerned about the negative impacts of fracking that she decided to do something about it. Over some months she showed the film to friends and then through the internet found a small group in her area with similar concerns that was just beginning to meet.*

These five people organized themselves so well that in the 2012 election, thanks to good coaching from more experienced groups elsewhere, their proposal to ban fracking from their city won by a wide margin despite a well-funded campaign to defeat it. This small group used their collective power with great skill. Said Judith, "I had no idea when we began that so few people could have such an impact and even be recognized all over the country as a model for initiating and making governmental change."

Here's a summary of the differences among the first three kinds of power we have described in this chapter. Note that *all* forms of power can be used negatively or positively.

PERSONAL POWER (PP)	ROLE POWER (RP)	STATUS POWER (SP)
• PP is our birthright. It is our individual ability to have an effect or to have influence. • It is accompanied by the inherent human right to be treated with dignity, respect, and fairness. • Although PP is always present, we can be more or less aware of it and have more or less access to it. • Our PP can be limited by ourselves and by the misuse of power by others, but in most situations we can retain some PP through positive attitudes and self-respect. • We can learn to use our PP better in both up-power and down-power roles. • PP comes in many forms, including the power of communication (articulateness), presence (charisma), and creativity.	• RP, or Positional Power, is earned, awarded, or assigned. Thus it is also called Assigned Power. • RP is separate from our PP and is thus mutable. It automatically accompanies any assigned position. • RP carries an increased or expanded amount of power and responsibility. • It is often integrated with PP. • Up- and down-power dynamics creates the need for ethical guidelines. • Some assigned roles carry greater increased power and responsibility; in such cases it will likely have a greater negative or positive impact on others. <u>Examples:</u> Doctor/Nurse Teacher/Principal Coach Employer Clergy Chairperson Therapist/Social worker Elected Official Chief Executive Officer Supervisor Famous Person Parent Director Bodyworker Policeman/woman	• SP is the increased power and influence ascribed to certain inherited characteristics by a society. • SP entails responsibilities, dynamics, and influence that often go unrecognized. • The impact of SP is often more subtle than that of RP. Those with high SP are often unaware of this fact. The fish, according to the saying, are the last to know they are in water. • SP depends on cultural values. Thus it may change from culture to culture. <u>Examples:</u> Age Wealth Education Race Sexual Orientation Nationality Gender Physical Appearance Physical Prowess Religious Affiliation Social Class

Sources of Power

Where do our various kinds of power come from? Beyond the obvious positional power granted by others to individuals like police officers, governors, ministers, or doctors (RP) or through deference shown to the wisdom, presence, or communication ability of others (SP), the answer is elusive. Some believe that power comes from the Almighty—Note the name.—and that everything anyone does results from God acting through them. Others believe that their personal power is the result of good genes, excellent education, ongoing self-development, and will power. There are, of course, other beliefs about the source of power. Whatever our belief, we can take it as an excuse to misuse our power or a resource for using it wisely and well. Thus it is important to name and acknowledge our experience of source while realizing that others may base their ideas of power on different sources.

To conclude, while power is neutral, it can be used and misused in many ways. Moreover, it comes in different forms. The good news is that knowledge is power too. Therefore, the first thing we need to understand is that we all have power, there are different kinds of power, and the main issue is whether we understand the power we have, how power works, and are able to use it to benefit all who are touched by it, including ourselves. The rest of this book will help you learn how.

Chapter 2:

Negotiating Power Differences

RIGHT USE OF POWER

CHAPTER 2:

Negotiating Power Differences

Power differences are a fact of life. Try this: *Using your imagination or actually moving around, think about walking with someone in a position of authority over you—a teacher, doctor, therapist, police officer. Notice whether your way of walking differs from your normal walk. People in our classes say things like: "Wow. My shoulders are a little more rounded. I feel more timid. I'm really alert and watching." Now, shift to imagining that you are walking with someone over whom you have authority. What changes? We've heard responses such as: "I feel taller and more sure of myself. My focus is totally on the other person. I feel responsible for their care." Now, shift and imagine walking with a peer. "I'm much more relaxed and at ease. There is less focus. Everything is easier."* Power differences of all kinds can show up in our bodies even when no words are exchanged.

Personality differences can cause perceptions of differences in power. For example, an extrovert in Western cultures is usually given credit for having more personal power than an introvert. Other power differences come from status. For example, a rich, white, educated, heterosexual is seen as having a high level of power just because of his status.

The differences in power in a relationship—what we call the Power Differential—requires the up-power person to be careful not to abuse or misuse his or her power. In fact, the potential impacts of this power differential create the need for ethical codes and guidelines to prevent harm by the person in the up-power role toward the one down-power. We call a role *up-power* because the person (doctor, priest, CEO, social worker) has greater influence, authority and responsibility than those in *down-power* roles (patient or nurse, parishioner, employee, client). As a result, those down-power are more vulnerable in a number of ways.

Here's another process for you to try:

Imagine you are a king or queen. One of your subjects pleads for the release of his brother from prison. Now, you have the power to say yes or no, and your subject will have to live with your answer whatever it is. Notice how you feel having this kind of power. Now, imagine you are the subject. You have a request which the king or queen can grant or deny on a whim or after thoughtful reflection. How do you feel in this down-power position? This level of power-over is widespread in today's world, although the up-power person is more likely to be a branch manager than a king or queen. The existence of power is NOT the problem. Rather, abuse of power comes when it is used with little or no skill, compassion, sensitivity, or wisdom.

The Power Differential Is Useful and Often Essential

The power differential is not just a given; it is often useful. You don't want to consult a psychotherapist who tells you her problems as if you were best friends. You also want to be sure that your doctor has had the proper medical training and knows what he's talking about. You want your employer to be keeping the health of the company in mind at all times. You want a policeman to take charge and be trained to prevent harm or stop violence. The increased power and responsibility of up-power people is meant to guarantee

- safety and security,
- confidence in the up-power person's knowledge, training, and expertise,
- direction and support,
- clear role boundaries, and
- appropriately shared responsibilities.

The assigned power differential works for the benefit of both sides in such relationships so long as both understand and feel empowered in their roles. When we go to see a doctor, we are in a vulnerable place. We are in some way not well. We count on the doctor to be able to figure out what's wrong and what to do about it. Empowered in our down-power role, we arrive at our appointment with information the doctor might need, relevant questions, and a willingness to let her guide us. The doctor, empowered in her up-power role, is confident in her expertise and respects and uses the information we give her about ourselves to form a diagnosis and treatment plan.

Story: *Cedar took her 91-year-old mother to a doctor's appointment. Knowing that she gets nervous in medical offices, Cedar helped her mother write down all her symptoms. "Here's a copy for you of all the information I have as well as four questions for you," she told him. The doctor, who was warm and reassuring, looked at the information, examined her, asked a few questions, and then spoke directly to her. "Thank you for bringing me so much information. Here's what I think. . . . How does this idea sit with you?" Both my mother and the doctor were using their down- and up-power roles well. This is how such interactions are supposed to work and often do.*

Although each of us has the capacity for wise, skillful uses of the power differential, we have all been wounded by misuses or abuses of power on the part of those in positions of authority. News media are full of stories of such harm. We and our friends have our own personal stories. Such horrific, painful, and sensational stories get the most airtime. The news in this regard is often bad.

We want to talk now about the kinds of misuse of power that can be prevented by understanding the dynamics of the power differential. First, let's share a bit about the under-use of power.

"Not power over, but power with" and *"shared power"*: We've heard these phrases so often that they have become clichés for correcting all we consider wrong with power. Yes, what's wrong with how many people use power needs to be corrected. Unfortunately, these phrases are not only misleading but contribute to another kind of misuse of power: its under-use. Let us explain.

Over the past 30 years or so, there has been an important shift in both personal and professional settings from the huge differences in power between Doctor and Patient, Therapist and Client, Employer and Employee, Clergy and Parishioner, Teacher and Student, Parent and Child. Consider how in the decades immediately after World War II, children were always taught to call any adult Mr., Mrs., or Miss. In present-day America, by contrast, kids routinely address adults by their first names. Or, in the traditional view, the Doctor knew all while the Patient knew nothing; the Therapist would put together a diagnosis without input from the Client; the Parents (often the Father) would make all the decisions for the Children; and the Teacher would rap knuckles or shame Students in front of their peers. The down-power person is subject to the will of the authority.   The up-power role has "power over" the down-power role. Much harm has been and is still being caused by this dynamic.   "Power over" has come to mean manipulation, abuse, force, disrespect, exploitation, and oppression.

Story: Sensitive, caring people don't want power over. They strive for equality—a "power with," or "shared power." As a consultant, Cedar once worked with a small company troubled by disorganization. She asked the employees to think of the conference room as a kind of map of their organization and to move to where they felt they were in relation to each other. The room was quite chaotic for a number of minutes. Having noticed that the CEO had moved to a far corner and sat down, Cedar quietly suggested that she see what would happen if she got up and moved to the center of the room. Astonishingly, when she did so, everyone else knew where they should stand, and the chaos in the room diminished. The CEO had wanted everyone to feel equal but in the process had abandoned the requirements of her role. By having effectively abdicated her place in the company hierarchy, she had unwittingly done away with the natural, useful differences between people inherent in their positional roles. As chief executive officer she had a role that carried with it increased power and responsibility. She needed to stand in her personal power and at the same time understand and own the additional power, influence, and responsibility that she had said yes to when she accepted the job. Cedar later heard that the CEO had become a more assertive leader and that the company's productivity had increased as a result.

Although the CEO in the story was right that all human beings deserve to be treated with dignity, all roles are not created equal. There are multiple differences. Those in up-power roles get paid more, can hire and fire, assess results, and are responsible for success and for maintaining a larger vision of their work.   These differences require experience, training, and maturity.   Hierarchy is not the enemy, just as power isn't.   Hierarchy is useful for task accomplishment, safety, role clarity, and good boundaries. It's the misuse of hierarchy that leads to the misuse of power. The increased power and responsibility of the up-power person is, in fact, "power over"–something that can and should be used for achieving goals in the interest of all.

Sensitive, caring people can make mistakes by not understand or owning their role power. Do any of these descriptions fit you?

• Believing in equality, you find it difficult to accept that your role creates a power differential with those who report to you and that this inequality is actually essential to your effectiveness.

• Rushed for time, you underestimate the power differential and over-focus on information and the accomplishment of tasks without noticing relationship issues and stresses as they emerge.

• In fear of manipulative and wounding abuses caused by being in charge, you don't own the power you have in order to use it for good.

• Considering your increased power as proceeding from *self* rather than *role*, you inadvertently dis-empower, disregard, or disrespect those down-power from you.

• Motivated by a desire to be of service and not cause harm, you don't see that your impact may be different from your intention and that your actions may be experienced as confusing or harmful.

Over the past 40 years many people and organizations have been attempting to empower minorities, employees, clients, and those who have been oppressed or exploited. This is a good thing but not at the cost of disowning the existence and importance of the power differential and refusing to invest time and energy into learning how the dynamics between up- and down-power roles work.

Here's a chart that describes role differences and their accompanying responsibilities. In this discussion of power-over and power-with, the up-power column describes the ways in which up-power people have *power over* those down-power from them. The lack of recognition and open acknowledgement of these essential power differences contributes to much confusion, dis-empowerment, and unnecessary suffering in role-power relationships in groups, businesses, and organizations of all kinds. Take a look.

ROLE DIFFERENCES AND
ACCOMPANYING RESPONSIBILITIES AND EFFECTS

(Reminder: We are all equal as human beings, have personal power, and deserve to be treated with dignity. Nevertheless, assigned roles come with increased power, influence, and responsibility.)

Person in the UP-POWER Role	Person in the DOWN-POWER Role
Is ultimately responsible for the whole or a larger part of the job/project/service.	Is responsible for his/her part of the job/project/service.

Has increased power and influence due to their responsibility to
• hire/fire/promote and demote;
• assess:
  progress/results/
  effectiveness/performance;
• prescribe or advise on tasks;
• deal with (personnel) problems;
• assign tasks/set standards and expectations;
• punish/reward down-power behavior;
• enforce rules;
• make final decisions
• .
	• Has decreased power and is vulnerable to being mistreated.
	• May feel less powerful as a person (not just in his/her role).
	• May have authority issues.
	• May have unrealistic expectations of the up-power person.
	• May assign the up-power person either more or less power than s/he actually has.

Receives higher pay and greater deference.	Receives lower pay and deference than up-power colleagues.
Sets and maintains appropriate boundaries.	Obeys or challenges boundaries as circumstances dictate.
Has greater influence through his/her words and actions.	Can be easily and strongly influenced by the words and actions of up-power persons. This influence can affect his/her dignity and self-esteem.
May have the role-related need to be liked or respected.	Has a role-related need or desire to be liked and respected.

Is less vulnerable to actions by those down-power from him/her.	• Has greater vulnerability to rejection, exploitation, disrespect, and manipulation than his/her up-power colleagues. • Risks more by giving challenging feedback, asking for change, or being assertive. •
Is 150% responsible for good relations and conditions. Note: The 150% Principle describes the extra relationship responsibility of up-power people.	Is 100% responsible for good working relationships and conditions and for resolving problems and conflicts.
May be easily idealized and/or devalued.	• May idealize, devalue, and/or have unrealistic expectations of the persons or groups in up-power roles; • Is more likely to escalate conflict when he/she doesn't feel heard or responded to or to withdraw and internalize his/her concerns.
May need to assist client/employee/family member in becoming more empowered, collaborative, respectful, engaged, inspired, confident, appreciated, and/or productive.	• May be disempowered or may unnecessarily dis-empower him-/herself and become lazy disrespectful, angry, unmotivated, passive, and unproductive; • May need to assist persons in up-power roles to use their power more wisely or skillfully.
May have difficulty understanding the difference and switching between interpersonally focused interactions and task-focused ones but is still 150% responsible for teaching and maintaining these two aspects.	May have difficulty understanding the difference and switching between interpersonally focused interactions and task-focused ones.

When in an up-power role, one needs to own their increased power, blend it with their personal power, and understand both how to use it well and how it can be misused. When one is in a down-power role, one needs to understand that down-power doesn't mean no-power. Power, as we've seen, is the ability to have an effect or to have influence. Even when in a down-power role, one still has personal power. So, one needs to own personal power and use it well, understanding the responsibilities held by up-power persons and the potential risks of harm that go with their positions. In a down-power role, one may even have opportunities to influence a system in which power is not being used well toward better uses of power.

What is important here is that we fulfill our power-over roles by understanding and becoming sensitive to the dynamics of power differences and by using our greater authority to empower those below us in ways that develop collaboration and support dignity. We must also fulfill our power-under roles by understanding and being sensitive to the dynamics of natural and assigned power differences and use our down-power roles in ways that foster collaboration and dignity.

We now want to talk further about a few of the relationship dynamics that are elicited by role-power differences.

Down-power does not equal no power.

While the above chart focuses on the responsibilities of the up-power (*power-over*) role and the special vulnerabilities of those down-power, we'd like to mention that what we've described is not black and white. Those in down-power roles also have role-related power they may or may not recognize and may use well or poorly. For example: They can quit. They can sabotage their boss. They can resist or complain to their boss's boss. They can make creative suggestions. They can exert positive influence for change. They can keep their own dignity and internal self-respect in spite of everything. They can join with others at their level and use collective power to bring about change. Likewise, those in up-power positions may have their own role-related vulnerabilities: for example, a dis-empowering misunderstanding of their responsibilities, an increased need to be liked or respected, unrealistic expectations, a crippling fear of criticism, or poor boundaries. Since all of us must navigate through both up-power and down-power roles in our daily lives, we need to be compassionate for ourselves and for others.

Projection

Projection is the subject of many books on psychology. We want to mention it here in the context of right use of power. Projection is the process by which we generalize from a situation in the past and transfer our understanding of that experience onto a current situation whether or not the new situation warrants it. *For example, because Bill's 6ᵗʰ-grade teacher under-used her power by not stopping the children in the class from laughing at and teasing Bill when he gave a verbal report, he projects and expects to be humiliated whenever he speaks in public. So, to prevent similar embarrassment, he avoids speaking up and experiences unnecessary suffering.*

Another aspect of projection consists of the processes of idealizing and de-valuing. We tend to project our expectations of perfection or ruthlessness on those in positions of authority. We imagine them to be flawless or abusive in their leadership. In the United States this phenomenon is typically seen in the reactions of citizens toward a new President. The former expect him or her to fulfill all their campaign promises perfectly and quickly despite the headwinds of politics. When the latter doesn't happen, disenchantment and even hatred can result. Or we idealize these up-power people, and then when they make even a small mistake, we completely devalue them. In reality, such leaders are generally neither super-heroes nor the scum of the earth.

Story: *Cedar once had a therapy client who placed Cedar on a pedestal. One day Cedar seriously misunderstood something at the end of the session and didn't notice that the client was upset. The client skipped her next appointment and even when Cedar called her to see how the relationship could be repaired, she was unwilling to return. Cedar guessed that when she didn't live up to the client's expectations, the latter felt she couldn't trust that the two of them would be able to resolve and repair the relationship. Perhaps she had decided never to try therapy again. Cedar, having made an unintentional mistake, was doing her best to take responsibility for it. The client for her part probably based her conclusion on past experiences with authority and then assumed the worst when she felt misunderstood and hurt by Cedar. She under-used her power by not responding to a genuine apology and offer of repair.*

Increased Risk

When we are in down-power roles, we have role-related vulnerabilities. We are at risk of losing our jobs or our projects. We are at risk of emotional harm from harsh criticism, disrespect, or humiliation. We are at risk of being exploited or oppressed. Something especially affected by this increased risk is our ability to give feedback.

Story: *Andre was a fifth-grade teacher in a small private school. Careful to be as tactful as possible and intending to initiate a conversation, he questioned the principal's judgment about one of his students. Several days later he was called into the office and told that he was being fired effective immediately. The feedback Andre gave was treated as insubordination. At this private school he had no recourse and had to leave.*

Whenever we ask in workshops how many people have experienced being treated unfairly or unjustly by a person in authority, almost everyone raises their hand. The need for experiential education about power issues is thus strong.

When we are in up-power positions, we should recognize that those down-power from us consider giving feedback, especially negative or even constructive feedback, as tantamount to challenging the competence of the leader. So, understanding the value of all kinds of feedback, we should use our authority to make giving feedback safe. We can do this by responding non-defensively, putting the feedback received to good use, and periodically asking for feedback that might not be easy for us to hear.

Influence

Story: *As a psychotherapist Cedar does a lot of mediation work. A couple came to her for couples' therapy. One of them said, "We went for one session to another therapist. She told us that our relationship was hopeless and that we ought to use therapy to help us get divorced! Can you believe she said that? We're really upset!"*

The couple did eventually get a divorce, but not before they had given the relationship their all in a number of therapy sessions. Since the therapist they were upset with was a colleague of Cedar's, Cedar decided to call her to find out what had happened in the session from her point of view. She had said it seemed there were some serious issues the couple would need to work on and that she, the therapist, wasn't sure whether they were coming to therapy to help save their marriage or to end it. The therapist, surprised to hear what the couple had taken from her words, was sad and upset. She hadn't realized what a powerful influence her words would have. By the way, this is also a situation in which her impact didn't match her intention, something we discuss in detail later in this book.

When we are in an up-power position, our words carry increased power to influence those down-power from us. A criticism or suggestion from a supervisor carries a lot more weight than the same comments would from a friend or colleague. Something meant as a casual comment by an up-power person can unexpectedly turn into a rule. Consider the following.

Story: *Sarah, the CEO of a non-profit, thought out loud in a staff meeting that perhaps there should be dancing at the next fundraiser. Her staff quickly instituted a plan for dancing as a necessary part of every future fundraiser. Sarah was amazed at the unexpected strength of her casual suggestion.*

The Need to Be Liked and Respected

Story: *A client once told Cedar, "When I was in the hospital, I did everything I could to be liked—by the nurses, doctors, everyone. I mean, to the extreme! I felt that if I didn't, they might not give me good attention. It seemed like my survival depended on being liked. I felt like I was a little baby again."*

There is a role-related increased desire and even a felt need for us to be liked by those up-power from us. This feeling is likely rooted in our early survival needs. For some, it is an increased need for respect. An excessively strong need for being either liked or respected is a danger signal indicating unconscious misuses of both down- and up-power. Wanting too hard to be liked may even lead an up-power person to try to be too agreeable and abandon the taking charge a situation requires. Wanting too hard to be respected, meanwhile, may cause an up-power person to be cold and unapproachable. A high need for being liked, moreover, may lead both an up-power and down-power person to get involved in a sexual affair. Although the attraction may be mutual, the up-power person who must guard the safety and good boundaries of all relationships bears the ultimate responsibility for their health. This is an example of our 150% Rule, which we'll describe more fully below. After all, the down-power person is the more vulnerable of the two.

Story: *"Yes, I liked him, but in retrospect, it was more that I liked the status of being his lover. But he implied that I would lose my job if I didn't go along with it. I needed him to like me. In the end, even though I agreed to it, I felt completely violated and taken advantage of."* The up-power person's response by contrast was, *"I thought she liked me. When she betrayed me, of course it wouldn't work for her to be in that job anymore."*

Cedar's client was in great distress: she had just lost her job. The up-power person completely didn't "get" what his responsibility was and how the dynamic worked. Cedar's client got used and unjustly punished. A traumatic misuse of power happened here, and the up-power person did not recognize or take responsibility for the impact of his role-related power. In this case there was human but not role equality.

Task- and Relationship-Oriented Interactions

In any kind of organization (business, family, church, office) there are two kinds of interactions: those related to the getting the task done and those related to maintaining good relationships. The interactions, different in each case, can be confusing when you don't understand the difference.

Story: *Juan felt he had a great relationship with his boss. They had good, supportive conversations at work, even about personal matters. Juan was thus quite upset when his boss didn't consult him before making a decision about a task Juan was working on. Su Lin was known for her no-nonsense efficiency in getting tasks completed. She was genuinely surprised when her staff began grumbling behind her back and becoming insensitive to each other. Juan thought that since he felt interpersonally close to his boss, he would be consulted about every business decision. Su Lin thought that since her team was getting the job done, there wouldn't be any interpersonal frictions. Juan did not understand that in his down-power role he would need to be able to honor and adjust to his boss's up-power task and decision-making responsibilities and not feel personally slighted. Su Lin for her part did not understand that relationship-nurturing interactions are necessary to help work teams complete their tasks.* *

Who is most at risk of harm?

When in an up-power position, we must hope that those down-power from us will use their role wisely and well. However, many of us in down-power positions forget that up-power is only a role-related add-on and unnecessarily give up our personal power. We need to keep our personal power intact to remain empowered in our down-power roles. It is good to remember that those most vulnerable to harm, even unintended harm, are those who

- lack personal awareness,
- are not relationally skilled,
- are impaired by pain or anxiety, and/or
- have low self-esteem.

Power-Differential Responsibilities

All assigned roles have responsibilities. Here is a list of some of them. The sensitivity and wisdom with which these responsibilities are assumed by those up-power are the major determinants of how healthy a

*See Nevis, Backman, and Nevis, "Connecting Strategic and Intimate Interactions: The Need for Balance. " (Gestalt Review, 7(2):134-146, 2003).

work environment will be and how well those down-power will be able to respond to their leaders.

Some Common Power-Differential Responsibilities are

- setting and maintaining appropriate boundaries;
- creating a sense of safety in work or other environment;
- staying in charge while remembering to be compassionate;
- protecting confidences and being trustworthy;
- holding and communicating a vision that gives context to the organizational goals;

- being sensitive to potential impacts on those down-power;
- inviting and being responsive to feedback;
- assessing and appropriately sharing results;
- keeping accurate records;
- empowering and collaborating with down-power team members;
- being fair and non-defensive; and
- applying the 150% Principle (which we shall now discuss).

The 150% Principle

One of the most important and comprehensive ideas we want to convey is the concept that while both members of an up-power/down-power relationship are 100% responsible for the health of the relationship, the person in the up-power role is 150% responsible. Over and over we hear remarks like the following from up-power people: *"Well, what could be wrong? The sexual liaison was completely mutual." "My employee created the problem, not me." "He's the one who's difficult to talk to." "He's always resistant." "We're all equals, so I don't see why I need to bring this situation up."* These responses represent a lack of understanding by supervisors of both the normal vulnerability of those in down-power roles and the extra responsibility for handling people and problems that is a natural part of being up-power.

Reynold Ruslan likens this situation to a boat, where the up-power person has a motor while the down-power person has only an oar. In this analogy, the person with the motor must be extra-careful not to overpower the person with the oar. Moreover, the former must be careful not to injure the latter with his more powerful tool.

Here then are some things that may be surprises in using your power wisely and well:

• The relational impacts and responsibilities differ for those in up-power and down-power positions.
• Our daily lives move us back and forth between up-power and down-power roles so we must remember to make appropriate changes in our behavior. An African proverb puts it well: *When the music changes, so does the dance.*

Chapter 3:

Increasing Your Awareness and Sensitivity

RIGHT USE OF POWER

CHAPTER 3:

Increasing Your Awareness and Sensitivity

*I'm trying to imagine being ethical without an awareness of my power.
That would be like trying not to step on anyone's toes without an
awareness of one's feet.* (Susan Mikesic)

Connecting our heart with our power—in both up- and down-power positions—involves increasing our personal awareness and sensitivity. Finding out more about our feet, in Susan's terms. This awareness includes understanding our history with people in authority and our beliefs about power and its impact on us and others.

Curiosity

Let's start with our history, since for better or worse it follows us around. First, though, a little bit about curiosity. Curiosity is a misunderstood emotion or attitude (as in "curiosity killed the cat"), often relegated to children and childhood. When we explore our past experiences to understand their impact on our present life, curiosity turns out to be the best tool we can use—far more helpful than fear or blame.

Story: *Cedar asked students grouped into pairs to face each other and imagine there was a big conflict between them. Then she asked them to turn away from each other and change only ONE thing—to adopt an attitude of curiosity—and then, when facing each other again, to notice whether something was different for them. Here are some of their responses: "The whole situation was lighter." "Amazing! I'm now looking at my partner instead of at the conflict in the space between us." "My goodness, it [the conflict] doesn't seem impossible [to resolve] anymore."*

Curiosity, in other words, can be a game-changer. It's key to all the concepts and techniques we talk about in this book. Practicing being curious and surprised will add pleasure, depth, wisdom, and freshness to your personal and relational life. It's actually amazing how applying something as simple as curiosity can change everything in how we relate with one another.

Learning from Bad Experiences— Finding the Golden Thread

When invited to recall what they had learned from a time when they were wounded by someone in authority, students revealed some surprising things: *"I remembered something that happened when I was really young . . . , and as I followed this memory, I realized that the effect still causes ripples in my life. It was a memory of my second therapy session, when I was in 3rd grade. The therapist pulled out the wrong folder and called me by the wrong name. I was so uncomfortable but didn't know what to do. I didn't correct him and went back to class after the session. He realized his mistake soon after and offered a heartfelt apology. I never doubted his sincerity, but I've had a hard time forgiving him. Even now I feel a little bitter. As an adult, however, I know there is that same risk of being disappointed, but I know that I can say something if I'm called by the wrong name, and I no longer assume that other people [those in authority] don't make mistakes. Looking at the influence of power has given me another way to understand that incident—a small mistake made by someone with a power difference can feel pretty severe."*

Another student felt so shamed as a small child that she shut whole parts of herself away in her unconscious. As she was drawing a particular memory, she found herself making a red-and-black box and then folding the paper up as small as possible. As she told us the story, she began unfolding the drawing bit by bit. "I see now that I don't have to be ashamed anymore. I didn't do anything wrong. I can show myself and be bigger again. I protected myself well, but I am more powerful than I thought."

When we've been hurt, our bodies, minds, and spirits try to figure out how to make sense of the hurt and what to do to prevent something similar from happening again. When the event doesn't get successfully resolved or repaired, it's difficult if not impossible to understand what really happened. So we make things up. Especially when we are young, we have little access to more complex explanations.

In this memory exercise, the students realized that they had made some big assumptions about power based on painful personal experiences. *"I decided that power was bad and I wouldn't have anything to do with it." "I decided I had to be stronger and meaner than anybody else to protect myself from getting hurt." "I decided it wasn't safe to say what I felt." "My brother was really mean to me, and I decided just to go inside myself and not respond to anything he did to try to get a rise out of me. It worked pretty well."*

The value of discovering these decisions that usually slip into unconsciousness is that by doing so, we can check them against reality, correct our understanding, and choose more effective responses in future. Cedar calls this "finding the golden thread." Here are a few "golden threads" named by the students quoted above. *"I see that I made a black-and-white decision about power and have avoided it to my detriment. I see that I can actually use my power for good. Who knew?" "I know I'm strong and can protect myself, so now I can risk letting myself have my softer feelings." "My golden thread is that [I know] I have now become super-sensitive to any kind of meanness—maybe too sensitive—so that I have trouble responding to conflict at all. I just pretend it isn't there."*

Here's another golden thread from a massage therapist: *"If someone had said to me fifteen years ago, after having been so wounded by sexual abuse, that I would today be using my hands for healing, I would have said, 'How is this possible?' I would have been bound by fear. But the power of grace is that often there is a gift in the wound that can open into the very gift we are to bring to others."*

You can try this memory exercise on your own. There are instructions and a blank grid to fill out in the "Try This" section at the back of the book.

Getting to Know Yourself Well Enough

Knowing your own history in relation to authority and your personal power is essential for learning to use your power wisely and well. It will help you be more aware of and sensitive to your own processes and your impact on others. It will also help you understand when relationships get confusing. And, as the following story illustrates, it will assist you in knowing yourself well enough to prevent possible harm in future.

Story: *Jamie chronically misused her power by employing her well-honed ability to figure out exactly what to say and not say to her husband. This practice resulted in her being secretive about her own feelings and needs. She was scared that some aspect of herself might be rejected if she revealed too much. She came to therapy because she wanted to be able to express more of herself and be "bigger." As she was talking about the most recent incident, Cedar noticed her hands speaking for her. Cedar asked her to focus on her hands: "My right hand is clamping down on my left hand. . . . [It's] a lot of pressure!" Cedar then invited both her hands to "speak": "My right hand is strong and controlling. It says, 'I won't let you say that, because then you'll get hurt. You are really weak and stupid, and you make mistakes.'" How does your left hand respond? Cedar asked. After a long silence, Jamie replied, "I hate it that you are so controlling. You won't let me do anything. It's not fair." After Jamie had reflected, she found that her left hand was able to demonstrate it actually was strong, resilient, and intuitive. The two sides began to explore how they could work together so that there would be room for both of them. Jamie began to use these insights pro-actively by asking her protective side to withdraw for a bit so that she could speak up for herself and her needs in the knowledge that the protective side would help her be resilient.* (Note: This story resembles that of Maria in Ch. 1.)

Another realm where we can become more sensitive and aware is our culture-based beliefs. We have unconsciously absorbed many messages about power and how to use it from our culture. Messages often differ from one culture to another, so we are sometimes surprised or even shocked by the behaviors of others that are appropriate to their culture but not ours. For example, when Cedar first taught in Japan, she expected her students to take an active part in class discussions. But for the Japanese, offering personal opinions and responses is seen as not being respectful to the teacher, a personage held in high esteem. Moreover, speaking up may even be considered showing off and shaming one's peers. The Japanese proverb makes the point succinctly: The nail that sticks out gets hammered in.

Take a minute now to identify a few messages about power that come from your cultural background. Pick one or more and respond to items A - D. You can fill out a version of this chart in the "Try This" section at the end of the book.

CULTURE	MESSAGE
• Class • Sex • Nationality • Race • Age • Education • Employment	A. MESSAGE received about power. B. HOW does this message affect how I use my personal and/or role power? C. Have these messages caused me to feel DISEMPOWERED? D. What are some NEW WAYS OF THINKING, FEELING, OR BEHAVING that might help me mediate the impact of these beliefs and make me feel more powerful?
Sex: Female	One person's responses: A. "I received the message that women should stay in the background and support men, so B. I'm reluctant to take charge or be directive when I'm in an up-power position. C. Obviously, I feel disempowered most of the time when in the company of men. D. I can understand that this is a cultural, not factual, belief and begin experimenting with putting myself forward more and learning to discern what situations will be most supportive of my new behavior."

Healthy Boundaries

Good boundaries are a centerpiece for safe, successful relationships. Setting clear boundaries is an engaging, often challenging arena to practice linking our strength with our compassion. But let's start with a definition. *Boundaries* are the psychological and physical space that people consider part of their identity. It's comparable to the three- or twelve-mile limit that countries bordered by oceans consider their sovereign territory in the sea. Our skin, for example, is our physical boundary. Some people are less welcoming to touch than others. Individuals also have energetic and emotional boundaries. Inadvertent boundary crossings can be upsetting. Boundaries, which vary from person to person, can be negotiated between people—often non-verbally. As the anthropologist Edward Hall pointed out in his book *The Hidden Dimension* (1966), comfortable communication distances differ for persons from different cultures. As a generalization, he found that individuals from Mediterranean cultures preferred to stand closer to their interlocutors, while those from Northern Europe required greater distances. Hence in the Seinfeld TV series, one hears about "close speakers" and "far speakers."

Story: *Hall mentioned a scene he witnessed at an embassy party in Athens, Greece, where a British and a Greek diplomat were having a conversation. The Greek felt too far from his British colleague to speak comfortably and kept trying to get closer, while the Brit felt uncomfortable with how close his Greek colleague already was. As a result, the Greek kept moving in, while the Brit kept backing off. In effect, Hall commented, they were moving around the reception hall in a kind of cross-cultural* pas de deux.

Cultural differences notwithstanding, boundaries provide a psychological structure that defines, contains, and limits relationships while assuring comfortable interpersonal communications for the participants.

The Development of Boundaries

Boundaries are a fundamental aspect of human development. Infants are born into a swirling world of new sensations in which they experience no distinction between self and other—both are merged into one. Thus begins the universal and lifelong process of finding a Self, also known as individuation. Boundaries define and protect this process. They enable separation and can be negotiated for more intimacy in the creation of a healthy relationship. They in fact empower us by providing appropriate limits.

Healthy boundary development proceeds through stages, briefly described here by our Boulder colleague Mukara Meredith* as

1) "**Undifferentiated**," *with the need to feel welcome and secure in our caregiver's charge.*

2) "**Separate but Surrounded**," *with the need to receive support and nourishment.*

3) "**Open Support**," *with the need to develop autonomy by coming and going from our caregiver's protective presence.*

4) "**Overlapping**," *with the need to be able to say no and still belong,*

5) "**Individuated**," *with the need to join and separate, be creative and unique, without fear of losing love.*

*(For more information on Mukara's teachings, see MatrixWorks.org.)

Boundary Styles

To various degrees in our self-development, all of us in both up- and down-power roles have experienced challenges and wounds. We consequently adopt boundary styles that, although designed to be protective, may actually limit satisfying relationships.

Relationship-limiting styles include over-bounded, under-bounded, and pendulum styles. Experientially, being **over-bounded** is an "automatic no" style. Relationships are compromised because there is no way to get close to an over-bounded person. As John Bradshaw says, "*There's no door knob to the self.*" Those with this boundary style have difficulty letting go, softening, nourishing, or being nourished. Over-protecting themselves because of a fear of being hurt, they are out of touch with their ability to be resilient and appropriately protective. Experientially, being **under-bounded** is an "automatic yes" style. Relationships here are compromised because the individual has little sense of the other. Good relationships actually *thrive* in the negotiating of differences. Users of the under-bounded style feel so frightened of being abandoned that they lose touch with their Self in the illusionary belief that there will then be nothing for others to reject. They feel confused about what they want or need and try to merge with others. Those who use the **pendulum style**, finally, veer back and forth between being over-bounded and under-bounded. This style compromises relationship by being unpredictable

Healthy Power Zone Boundaries

Take a moment to reflect on your boundaries. Where would you place yourself on the following continuums? Living in the Power Zone is reflected in placement within the gray area on these continuums. Remember that the Power Zone is a healthy range of your responses, rather than a "dead center" spot. Power Zone responses are flexible and and appropriate within this gray range. What matters most is being able to respond well in individual relationships and situations.

Over-bounded automatic no		Under-bounded automatic yes
Not enough differentiation		Not enough integration
Inflexible		Elusive
Controlling		Easily controlled
Rigid		Merged
Uncompromising		Vague and confused

Just Say Yes or Just Say No.

The simplest place to begin working with your boundary style is with yes's and no's. If you have an "automatic no" style (over-bounded), practice saying more yes's. Perhaps you could experiment with one conscious "yes" a day. Notice if your conscious yes results in a sense of losing yourself. The ability you want to develop is to be able to say yes and still be yourself. (Of course, there are times when it is right to "merge.") If you have an "automatic yes" style, you could experiment with one conscious "no" a day. Then notice if the result of the no is disconnection from the other party or the group. The ability you want to develop is to be able to say no and stay connected. (And of course, there are times when it is necessary and right to speak a firm no as a way to disconnect from an inappropriate situation.)

Story: *Cindy has an automatic-yes style. She wants to be helpful. She wants to be liked. She doesn't want to disappoint anyone. So she automatically says yes to almost everything. She has too many projects she's working on, too many friends to stay in touch with, and too many commitments. She works too many hours and has too little fun. She suffers from burn out. Her therapist asked her in the session to spend a few minutes practicing saying no, finding out how it felt in her mouth, and how many ways she could do it—slowly, quickly, loudly, softly, clearly, vaguely. She then kept notes about her experience and the impact of each no she said. She was to say at least one no each day. "Yep, it looks so far like the world doesn't end when I say no. Some people appreciate that I'm taking care of myself. Some people are disappointed and upset. They need to get used to a different me. I'm relieved."*

Stage 2 for Cindy was to set some boundaries around her work life so it wouldn't be so overwhelming. She decided to limit herself to two hours of email work per day from 8:30 to 10:30 a.m. at a local coffee shop. Then she wouldn't look at email again until the next day. People wouldn't get instant responses anymore, but that aspect of her life would be more contained and less overwhelming. Then she set another time and place for two hours of writing each day—to focus and contain that aspect of her life.

Story: *Recently, our four-year-old goddaughter gave us some insight into how she was working out her boundary issues. Here's how it went.*

"Cedar, let's make an igloo!"

"Okay. How will we do that?" (With blankets over the couch and pillows as the block-ice walls, we made an igloo with a door that could be flipped open. We then nestled ourselves inside with a few books and a little drum. Rose then knocked her hand on the pillow wall.)

"I hear something. (Knocks again.) I hear something. Do you? What is it?"

"I don't know. What do you think?"

"It's wolves."

"Wolves! What do you think we should do?"

"Quick. Play the drum. That will keep them away. "She plays the drum and chants, "No, no you can't come in!"

"How is it working?"

"The wolf went away." (Knock, knock!) "It came back."

Again drumming: "No, no, you can't come in!" (We repeat this process five or six times, then . . .)

"Rose, how do you know if it is a friendly wolf or a mean wolf?"
(Pause)
"I know by how it knocks. If it knocks two times, it's a mean wolf, but if it knocks three times, it's a friendly wolf."
(Knock, knock!) "So this one's a mean one?"
"Yes. No, no you can't come in!"
(Knock, knock, knock!) "It's a friendly wolf! Open the door and let him in!"
(Down comes the igloo, and suddenly the game is over.)

Rose is involved in play at pre-school with many different children. She's learning that she can make her own choices about the children she wants to play with. She's learning how to discern who's friendly and who's mean by their actions or attitudes. She's learning that she can have a strong effect: she can actively include or exclude others by her tone of voice, choice of words, and determined attitude.

Generally, we are looking to make discerning choices rather than automatic ones. We want to be able to say yes's and no's that are strong, compassionate, and appropriate. As our colleague Dyrian Benz puts it, *The task is to recognize our interdependence, honor boundaries and differences, and remember connectedness.*

Intention and Impact

"I don't need to learn about power or sensitivity or ethics. I have good intentions. I don't want to harm anyone. That's all I need, my good intentions." This is a common misunderstanding. We have heard it from good people everywhere. Surely we want to applaud good people with good intentions. Indeed, good intentions are the foundation of good work and relationships. However, we want to tell you a few reasons why good intentions are necessary but not sufficient for using our power wisely and well.

The most important reason is that our impact doesn't always match our intention. Ironically, our impact is often quite different from, even the reverse of, our intention. Here's an example: Our desire to express support for someone's improvement ("Your presentation needed more clarity.") might be heard by the individual as harsh and critical. Up-power people often forget how easily a simple statement may have unintended consequences. And just think how often couples get upset with each other because the impact of their words is different from their intention. To cite an instance, one partner, skilled in active listening, intended to demonstrate he had heard by repeating the other partner's phrases or ideas before speaking his own. His partner, however, experienced this habit as a sign of disrespect by taking her words and making them his own. This problem took a while to resolve until both partners came to understand the difference between intention and impact.

Impact *is the effect your behavior has on others.* Intention *is the effect you want it to have.*

One of the reasons our impact may not match our intention is that, as mentioned in Chapter 2, we all have our own history. In fact, we see things not as they are but as *we* are. In other words, we hear words and experience behavior through our own personal filters. If we are sensitive to criticism, we may tend to experience comments from others as critical even when they are not. When impact and intention don't match, what's important to realize is that both people are right. The intender is being true to her intention even as the receiver is being true to his. There's no need for either to be defensive or insist on being the one who's right.

This is another situation in which curiosity is the best tool to use. Either party to the interaction, or both, could become curious. What did the other person "make up" that you said or did? What did the other person really intend?

The Five-Keys Process

You may find this simple five-step process useful for preventing or remedying impact-and-intention discrepancies.

1. **Sensitize** yourself to the possibility that your impact was different from your intention.
2. **Listen** to the other's experience. (*"Please tell me about your experience just now."*)
3. **Validate** the other's experience. (*"I can understand how you could feel hurt."*)
4. **Explain** your intention in a simple way. (*"It wasn't my intention to hurt you. My intention was _____."*)

5. **Ask** what else is needed. (*"How are you feeling now?" Or, "Is there anything else you need around this?" Or, "How are we doing now? Do we need to do anything else to repair our relationship?"*)

Tracking for and identifying an inappropriate or distorted impact can help correct a relationship quickly and successfully. As in sailing, the person at the helm keeps the goal in sight but may have to tack back and forth across the wind to reach it. Similarly, the journey to a deep, lasting relationship is seldom a straight cruise to the horizon. More frequently, the partners must engage in periodic self-correction. A word of caution: A big self-correction takes a lot more effort than a little one, but too many tiny and time-consuming corrections can slow the process of relating to a snail's pace. Fortunately, one can learn from experience how to get things just right.

Increasing our awareness and sensitivity in relationships—be they up-power, down-power, collegial, or between friends—essentially calls for becoming interested and engaged in the on-going process of studying and refining our impact on others. This habit will lead to a greater congruence between our intention and impact and also to our being able to repair relationships when differences come up.

Tracking Skill

How do you study your impact? Sometimes your impact is obvious, as when someone gets angry at you. Sometimes the impact is subtle and requires more careful attention. We call this skill "tracking." Tracking is the moment-to-moment process of noticing another's responses to what is said or done or to their expression of feeling. These responses will be visible or felt through their tone of voice, body movements, words, gestures, facial expressions, or other physical manifestations. The latter can be quite subtle (For example, an emotion if unnoticed and unacknowledged disappears in a few seconds.) or quite obvious, as in

changes in body language such as folding arms, looking away, or tears.

Contacting Skill

"Making contact" is the process of verbally or non-verbally letting another know that we understand and are present with them. Nodding, smiling, saying short phrases like "I get it," "I understand," "Tell me more," "This must be painful for you," or "I didn't understand what you just said; please say it again" are all "contact" sentences. Tracking and contact go together like bread and butter. You will find these skills to be of immense value in using your power and influence well.

Housekeeping Skill

Housekeeping is the process of keeping a relationship clear and productive. Just like houses, relationships need periodic cleaning—airing out, dusting, fixing a stuck window, or stopping a water drip. It's no big deal, neither good nor bad. There's just some attention needed. If you break an egg on the floor, you clean it up. If there is a break or lack of clarity in the relationship, you clean it up. (Tracking, contacting, and housekeeping are techniques that come from the Hakomi Method of Psychotherapy. See see www.hakomiinstitute.com.)

Returning to the 150% Principle we learned about in the last chapter, the person in the up-power role has 150% responsibility for holding the boundaries, attending to safety, resolving and repairing emerging difficulties, and keeping the relationship healthy.

Story: *Russ Lucero is a school bus driver. On January 18, 2013, he received one of the five coveted Impact Awards from the Boulder Valley School District. Russ uses riddles, guessing games, and a word-of-the-day to keep kids learning even before and after they're in the classroom. "I get these kids twice a day for fifteen minutes, and I have an incredible time with them. I connect with them, I listen to them, and I put their welfare first."* (Alex Burness, "One Fine Day" *Boulder Daily Camera*, 1/19/13) Here, Russ's impact clearly matches his intention, and he demonstrates his awareness of and sensitivity to the needs and interests of his riders and uses his up-power role to give his riders more than just a bus ride.

Pepe Salazar after one of our workshops said, *"No longer am I just a movement therapist who wants to help people. I am a leader. I am becoming a model for how to use power wisely, consciously, and with skill. I understand that it's not good enough to just be a good person and have good intentions. I must be myself in my own powerful way that does more than not do harm, but rather stays in right relationship with others and repairs harm while teaching them by example how to use their power benevolently."*

Chapter 4:

Living in the Power Zone

RIGHT USE OF POWER

CHAPTER 4:

Living in the Power Zone

Cedar once had a dream in which she picked up a book that started in the middle and moved toward the outside pages like an expanding spiral. Our logo and cover design provide an illustration of this idea. Now here we are in the middle of this book, and, as in Cedar's dream, it is the core of everything else.

That core is what we call **living in the power zone**. It has three aspects. One is to learn to balance power with heart in both down- and up-power roles. The second is to be able to stand in your strength while staying in your heart. The third is to become comfortable and adept at responding appropriately to situations within a healthy range of choices.

This concept of **power with heart** is a revolutionary idea. To embrace it, we need to follow a new paradigm—a socially intelligent model of power—in which we are not expected to choose between power as strength and power as compassion. Using power with heart is more challenging than either using power with strength or heart alone because to do so requires both resilience and vulnerability. The simpler, more extreme versions require neither.

Anodea Judith in *Waking the Global Heart* (2010) says, *"The organizing principle of the next era will be based on the power of love rather than the love of power, but humanity must undergo its initiation to adulthood in order to get there."* Learning to live in the Power Zone, we believe, is the major part of this initiation.

Power with Heart

Marc Ian Barasch's definition of compassion is *"resonating concern, an ability to see and respond to the connection between everyone and everything."* (*Field Notes on the Compassionate Life* (2005). So the first step in accessing power with heart is to take a brief "compassion training." Breathing in and out, make space inside to feel compassion. A lot of letting go, reorienting and changing of perspective can happen in even three breaths. Initially do this for yourself as you recall harm you may have caused, whether consciously or unconsciously. .Breathing in this way, Leela noticed: *I can sense that I am relating to compassion through my [mind]. . . . I can feel now that my heart center is ready to be cultivated. I will practice dropping my "home" from my head to my heart.* Also, practice feeling compassion for the inadequately trained leader who mistreated his followers, the dad who took out his marital unhappiness on his children, the teacher whose classroom behavior was affected by an unresolved wound from the past, or the doctor whose interaction with patients was unduly influenced by unmet personal needs. All of them misused their power. What they did created harm for others, but self-correction and amends can be made by anyone who truly wants to keep from causing additional harm in the future.

The power tools in each chapter of this book will help you achieve that goal. In fact, you will be able to prevent or repair harm and promote the general well-being. Good intentions are necessary but not sufficient to reduce the harm caused through naiveté, misunderstanding of the power differential, under-use of power, or kindness not balanced with strength. The good news is that you no longer have to be terrified of making mistakes, since almost all of them are reparable. The ideas in this book could be considered "power effectiveness training."

Power Without Heart Is Both Destructive and Common.

In the *Games People Play: The Psychology of Human Relationships* (1964), a book which would go on to sell over 5 million copies, Eric Berne described four kinds of interpersonal transaction: win/win, win/lose, lose/win, and lose/lose. In sports events, to be sure, each team strives to win. The successful one does, while the other side loses. With human beings, however, Berne argued that *both* the individuals and groups involved in an interaction needed to win for the long-term success of their relationship.

Several generations earlier, the German-Jewish philosopher Martin Buber wrote his famous essay "*Ich und Du*" (1923), "I and Thou." Buber's point was similar to Berne's. In too many human relations, Buber said, we do not treat the other person as a fellow "I," that is, as a "Thou."

Instead, we mistreat him or her as an "It." A mere ten years later, Hitler and the Nazis would come to power in Germany and tragically prove Buber's point.

When power is not used with heart, the likelihood is that it will result in win/lose relationships. To a greater or lesser extent the loser may be seen by the winner as a permanent loser, not as a fellow I to be empowered but as an It to be used and abused. Destructive relationships, psychological and physical abuse, and neglect can all result. The sum total of such dysfunction, then, is synonymous with the misery we see in the world.

In our workshops we invite people to try an experiment. In pairs they put their hands up and push each other's hands. They are instructed to be playful, not aggressive. They notice what the experience is like: "Fun, laughing, a bit scary because I was a woman with a man; energetic." Then they repeat the exercise, but this time they push hands with a feeling of compassion. "We were looking at each other this time and moving very slowly; almost nothing was happening, lots of warmth and personal connection." Then the third time, they put their hands together and push with both strength and compassion, power and heart. "Oh, right; this time there was energy and personal contact; something else was happening. The interaction had become collaborative."

You might want to try this experiment yourself with a friend. People tend to think, because of the effect of the dominant model of power, they have to choose either kindness or strength. Their concept is that power is harmful while compassion is helpful, or that the only way to get something done is to be strong and severe. In this exercise, they learn that if you just have heart and no strength, the relationship feels flat and lacks energy. But if you use only strength, you have no emotional connection and little ability to collaborate. If you look at extreme abuses of power, they happen when heart and strength are out of balance. Consider war on the one hand or chaos and neglect on the other. Everyday misuses of power reveal the same thing. Right use of power happens not in one specific spot on the continuum but within a healthy, flexible range. We call this range, as you now know, THE POWER ZONE. Here are some examples of the extremes on this spectrum:

OVER-USE OF POWER AS STRENGTH	UNDER-USE OF POWER AS COMPASSION
A parent severely disciplines a child.	An overly lenient parent spoils a child.
A teacher controls by intimidation/shame.	Wanting approval, the teacher loses control of the class.
A manager doesn't ask for feedback.	The manager refuses to manage.
An employer exploits his employees.	An employer doesn't ask enough of her employees.

The Earth Is Also a Thou.

Using power with heart goes beyond considering our impact on other human beings. Our brothers and sisters who are Buddhists or followers of tribal spirituality can help us understand that all sentient beings deserve to live as much as we do. We can practice considering ahead of time how our actions will affect the plants and animals, the soil, the sea, and the air. What impact will our decisions or lack thereof have on our children, grandchildren, and the generations beyond? As we used to say in the 1960s, not to decide is also to decide. When Lakota People in the Pipe Ceremony use the phrase "All my relations," they are including the Earth and all its vital contents. Everything for them is alive, and life by definition deserves our respect. We didn't create it, so we have no right to destroy it. On the contrary, we have an innate obligation to preserve and enhance it.

We Are All Role Models.

What we do or don't do, say or don't say, can have a permanent impact on someone else's life. Every one of us for better or worse is a role model for someone else. Consider Sir Paul David Hewson (b. May 10, 1960 in Dublin), better known as Bono. As lead singer and composer for the rock group U2, he used his fame as a springboard to activism and humanitarian work. Raising money through benefit concerts to combat AIDS, TB, and malaria in Africa, he would eventually be knighted by Queen Elizabeth II, nominated for the Nobel Peace Prize, and featured in 2005 as TIME's Person of the Year.

We mention him as an example of a celebrity using personal power for the greater good. Story: *Here is how Bono affected Dr. David Barstow, one of Cedar's brothers. A Ph.D. in computer science from Stanford University, Dave happened to attend a Bono benefit concert in Chicago some years ago. In the course of that event, the singer challenged his audience to follow his example of helping the less fortunate. That call began a process of reflection that led to Dave's retiring from consulting work—fortunately, he was able to do that—and turning his full attention to creating and growing EMPACT Africa (www.empactafrica.org). The purpose of Dave's nonprofit is to "empower pastors in sub-Saharan Africa to fight the HIV/AIDS pandemic by attacking the stigma and discrimination which are barriers to effective prevention and treatment." By the end of 2012 the organization had reached as many as one million citizens in southern Africa. Positive role models can be so powerful, and fortunately there are many other DavidBarstows out there who are hearing and following similar calls to service.*

Now, let's look at how we can bring together power with heart. We've talked about finding compassion for self and others. We've talked about operating in the healthy zone between the extremes of too much and too little power, too little and too much heart. (We are calling it Power with Heart, but really we mean power with strength and heart, because heart, or compassion, has PLENTY of power.) We've talked about doing the right thing, but doing it with skill and strategy. Finally, we've talked about being pro-active in preventing mistakes based on naiveté and lack of sensitivity and good tracking skills.

So, to summarize the fundamental ideas of power with heart and living in the Power Zone, it is a matter of living our life by bringing to bear all aspects of our self—our strength, compassion, wisdom, skill, and grace.

Power Parameters

Rather than being a monolithic force, power actually has many aspects. We call these power parameters. In our classes we put signs naming sets of opposite poles—one extreme on one wall; the other on the facing wall—and thus create a continuum between them. We then say, "*Please place yourself in the room where you feel you most often are on the continuum between over-using and under-using your power.*" People line up, and in the process a number of things become clear. *"Where I stand depends on who I'm with." "Not only that but it depends on what role I'm in." "I just can't do this—pin it down to one spot." "I see that I actually do have a habitual place. I'm an introvert, so I naturally gravitate to the under-use-of-power side on all of these because I'm shy and not easily out-going." "Hmmm. I'm an extrovert, and my personality leads me to the over-use side."*

Power, the ability to have an effect, can be directive or responsive, task-focused or relationship-focused, truth- or harmony-focused. We each have our most natural and comfortable forms for expressing these aspects. These habits in turn result from our personalities, upbringings, and cultures.

When we look at the entire range of each continuum, we find that misuses and abuses of power happen at the extremes. Extreme directiveness can produce a dictator, while extreme responsiveness can produce a pushover. An extremely task-focused person ends up burning out or having unresolved conflicts. Extreme relationship-focus, on the other hand, ends in a task left uncompleted.

To live in the Power Zone, you'll most likely need to expand your range so that you can more effectively respond to whatever situation you find yourself in. In the exercise just described, participants are subsequently invited to move slightly in the opposite direction and study what becomes possible for them in their new position. Responses we've heard include—*"Wow. I just moved a foot or so, and I feel somehow a little sturdier." "I don't like it. I'm not familiar [with being here], not comfortable." "Even though it feels a little out of character for me, I can see that being even slightly more directive with my employees could really help them focus on the job."* Then, whoever is facilitating walks in a circle that circumscribes a healthy range of responses short of the extremes and in so doing describes the Power Zone.

Responses now include things like *"Okay. I get it. There isn't only one right way. There's a whole range of right ways, and these depend on my personality and the situation I am in and who I'm dealing with." "I might in some circumstances have to pull back from my extroverted self in order to listen when it is important to listen." "I don't have to say, 'Hey, that's just the way I am'; I can stretch myself and see what happens."*

Of course, people exploring each parameter find that where they place themselves can vary by context: whether they are at work, home, with close friends or partner, etc. It's reassuring to discover that we already have a Power-Zone range. Story: *Our six-year-old goddaughter, Rose, gave us an example of stretching her range one afternoon at the jungle gym. She was not playing at either end of the zone. She wasn't being a daredevil taking dangerous risks, nor was she overly cautious by simply repeating what she already knew. She was trying to swing her feet up to the bar so that she could pull herself higher into the structure. She swung her feet and touched but couldn't quite hook her ankles over the bar. She tried a number of times. Then, when she had had enough of trying, she said, "Now I could use a little help." Next time she tries, we're pretty sure she'll make it to the very top.*

Story: *Surya was engaged in a distressing battle of wills with her 5 year-old-son. His temper tantrums were so severe that the only thing she could do to stop his rampaging was to buy him a toy that he wanted. With some guidance from the school counselor, she was able to expand her range of responses. First, moving to the compassionate side of the continuum, she began by telling him as she put him to bed, three things that she had appreciated about him that day. (At first, she had to look really hard to find three!) Then, moving toward the strength side, she told him that there were two things she expected of him: to go to school and to take a bath, and that his allowance was dependent on following through. The counselor made a few more suggestions, and in a remarkably short time, Panji was a different boy. "It's like we were in a constant head-on battle, and now we are going along side by side." Surya reported.*

We would like to invite you to try some experiments with going just a little beyond your comfort zone with these parameters. Here's a list of the ones we have identified.

- **directive/responsive**
- **firmly boundaried/flexibly boundaried**
- **task-focused/relationship-focused**
- **persisting/letting go**
- **truth-focused/harmony-focused**
- **strength-centered/heart-centered**
- **over-powering/under-powering**
- **extroverted/introverted**

You'll find a chart in the "Try This" section that you can use. As you consider each parameter, compare where you would put yourself in several contexts noted. Going into more depth about two of the power parameters will help explain two important principles for living in the Power Zone: blending power with heart and expanding your range of healthy responses.

The Extrovert/Introvert Parameter

The introvert/extrovert continuum is the "single most important aspect of personality," according to Susan Cain, who has put her extensive study of introversion into a book called *Quiet—The Power of Introverts in a World that Can't Stop Talking* (2012). Introversion and extroversion are very different expressions of power. It seems that extroversion is the modern American ideal. In schools, shy and quiet children are encouraged to be more outgoing. Shyness is seen as a sign of being wimpy, unsocial, and likely to become unsuccessful in life. Too bad, because, as Cain points out, by undervaluing introverts (who are at least one-third of our population), we fail to acknowledge that we owe them many of the great contributions to society—from Van Gogh's sunflowers to the invention of the personal computer. In addition to educational bias, she questions the dominant values of American business culture, where forced collaboration can stand in the way of innovation and where the leadership potential of introverts is often overlooked.

We mention Cain's insights because looking at the power-parameters chart, listed above, you'll notice that the items on the left side relate to extroversion while those on the right correspond to introversion. As novelist Edith Wharton puts it, "*There are two ways of spreading the light: to be the candle or the mirror that reflects it.*" Society needs both introverts and extroverts. (There is also a blended type in the middle called *ambivert*, referring to those who are comfortable on either side of the continuum.) In all the parameters, balance and a healthy range is the goal for using your power wisely and well.

Cain goes on to point out that introverts can most easily shift into extroverted behaviors when they are advocating for something they feel passionate about. An example is the interpersonally shy teacher who becomes dramatic and expressive when she gets in front of her class. Extroverts for their part can stretch into more sensitive and reflective behaviors too. It's a matter of valuing the other side of the polarity and trying it out for specific purposes.

 Story: *Cedar once asked an introvert/extrovert couple what they would suggest that the other do to relate more easily with them. The introvert had three suggestions: The extrovert should lower his voice to match hers. He shouldn't interrupt her. And he should wait one breath before responding. The extrovert offered this guidance: The introvert should give full, clear, and audible verbal responses. She should accept him as he was rather than trying to change him in some obvious way. And she should use lots of positive praise.*

 The key here for any of the parameters is balance and conscious stretching of our zone of comfort while remembering that violence happens at the extremes. There, people lose their heart connections to both themselves and others.

The Task-Focused/Relationship-Focused Parameter

 Being task-focused, according to Nevis, Backman, and Nevis, means having intentional interactions and making efforts to accomplish a task or achieve a desired goal—something they call "strategic interactions" ("Connecting Strategic and Intimate Interactions," 2003, *Gestalt Review*, 7(2): 134-146). Relationship-focused interactions are "behaviors and communications, verbal and non-verbal, that aim to enhance closeness and improve relationships." Nevis, Backman, and Nevis refer to these as "Intimate Interactions." Their list of qualities for both strategic and intimate interactions, as edited by C. Barstow, includes

Strategic, or task-focused, qualities:

- The ability to stay focused on a future goal without being deflected by emotions.
- Being abrupt, intrusive, or bold in the interest of time whether one is up-power or down.
- The ability of all members in a system to disagree or fight for alternatives and still maintain a hierarchical alliance.
- The understanding that hierarchy counts in decision-making: "As your father, I am responsible for you, and you are not getting the

car tonight." "Dad, that's not fair." "Perhaps not, but you are not getting the car."

- The ability to forgo a complete dialogue in order to enter into an action-based exchange.

Intimate, or relationship-focused, qualities:

- The ability to ask questions and give answers to learn more about each other's thoughts and feelings.
- The ability to commit to a sustained dialogue.
- Mutual involvement in influencing each other and being influenced by the other or others.
- The ability to stay focused on the here-and-now, the present moment.
- The ability to modulate the speed or tone of an exchange to accommodate to the rhythm of both parties.

These are obviously two modes of being in relationship. Both are important to the healthy functioning of couples, families, groups, and organizations. As the authors above note, living in the Power Zone in this parameter depends in effect on being able to understand the need for flexibility and then to shift modes in order to be kind, stay connected, and be able to work diligently together on a task. When using your power with heart, you will be blending these two modes, for you can be strong and compassionate in both.

Feedback as an investment in relationship

Feedback is any response, negative or positive, one gives to someone else about the impact of their behavior. Feedback could be about another's skillfulness, ideas, presentation, or style. As such, it must provide the individual with an opportunity to learn how others perceive their behavior or to let others know how they are perceived. The process of becoming more sensitive to one's impact is, naturally, a life-long engagement with power.

Feedback is aimed at fostering more awareness rather than getting another to change in accordance with our wishes or perceptions. In learning to live in the Power Zone, feedback is the single most important skill we can acquire. Whether positive or critical, it can be encouraging and well used when offered and received with compassion and respect. The most important thing is to give feedback in a way so that it can be received without damaging the relationship. Accomplishing this is a high-level skill. In fact, understood correctly, feedback, when properly offered, will turn out to be an investment in the relationship, a paradoxical concept we owe to Amina Knowlan.

Seeking and using feedback requires courage. It can feel to the individual like asking for trouble. Still, tactfully delivered feedback, even if critical, can

- encourage open and authentic communication;
- keep relationships current and alive;
- help us learn more about ourselves and our impact;
- prevent problems from developing;
- handle problems after they occur;
- deepen relationships;
- clarify relationship issues; and
- fine-tune the alignment between our intentions and our impact.

In short, the tool of giving and receiving effective feedback is fundamental to *staying* in the Power Zone.

Staying in the Power Zone by using feedback

We are including this point under the topic of using power with heart simply because giving effective feedback means thinking ahead of time how similar feedback would strike us if we were on the receiving end. It's a matter of applying the Golden Rule or putting ourselves in the other person's moccasins.

Let's face it. Whatever we do or don't do, say or don't say will strike others in positive or negative ways. Depending on how they relate to us, in other words, whether they are up- or down-power from us, will affect how their words impact us or vice-versa. A parent telling us they are ashamed of us will have one kind of effect. Another parent in the same situation saying they are proud of us, love us, and were wondering whether we had thought about other possible ways of treating our little sister will land in a totally different way. And as every pilot knows, the best landing is one you can walk away from without the feeling of never wanting to fly again.

Feedback tends to be feared and felt as criticism that will make us feel bad about ourselves, lose confidence, or require a big personal change. When feedback is perceived as negative, it's easy to see why we so easily feel defensive or hurt. Here's a new perspective, suggested above: *Feedback can be an investment in a relationship.* We can move from experiencing it as shudder and shrink to feeling it has improved our relationship. Our colleague Amina Knowlan says, "*Feedback is not a demand for change. It may be followed by a request for change, but the feedback itself is just data. . . . Feedback might be thought of as a way of 'lubricating' the channels of communication. . . . If, as Desmond Tutu says, 'We can only go forward together,' then feedback becomes a way of lending each other a hand.*

(For more information about Amina's teachings, see www.MatrixLeadership.org.)

The feedback process can be made more user-friendly when we think of it as four distinct activities:

Asking for Feedback

In *asking* for feedback you can take charge of the when, how, and what. That way you'll be more likely to hear and use it. Asking can also open the door to a deeper level of relationship.

- Be pro-active and if necessary ask often.
- Be specific. For example, "I'm curious about how you experience my _____ [Name the behavior.]."
- Tell the other person just how you'd like to receive the feedback—timing, pacing, balance of positive and negative observations, how much, etc.
- If it's an issue of particular concern, get feedback from more than one person.

Giving Feedback

Remember that here you are making an investment in the relationship. So be sure to offer the feedback in the way it can best be received.

- Ask first if the individual is willing to receive feedback and if now or another time would be more appropriate.
- Be compassionate, authentic, and courageous.
- Be concrete by using examples from the present or recent past.
- Suggest a specific behavioral change for the individual to try.
-

Receiving Feedback

Here again you can usually determine how and when you get the feedback.

- Suggest the parameters for timing, pacing, how much, and what kind.
- Be receptive, not defensive.
- Ask for clarification and examples as necessary.
- Respond in a way that encourages future communication.

Using Feedback

Just because someone gives you feedback doesn't mean that it's necessarily true or that you are required to do a personality makeover.

- If the feedback is new to you, check with several others to see if they agree with the feedback received.
- Remember that feedback is as much about the giver as you. Examine it critically before applying it.
- Experiment with applying a particular piece of feedback. Let's say the advice is to speak up more, try that behavior out and see how it works.
- Be appreciative by letting the giver know you are experimenting with some of his/her suggestions.

We consider learning to ask for, give, receive, and apply feedback the most important skill set for using power with strength and heart. It will help you keep relationships current, open, and authentic; learn more about yourself and your impact; prevent problems or help you handle them; clarify issues; and deepen relationships.

Being out of the feedback loop is one of the biggest causes of unintentional misuses of power. A manager refuses to listen non-defensively and loses a faithful employee or a good new idea. You can doubtless think of other illustrations of this point.

Story: *We all know the story of the Emperor's New Clothes. The Emperor is in a very up-power position. None of his subjects wants to embarrass him, or get their head chopped off for being the one to tell him the truth. So, the Emperor continues to strut down the street wearing nothing at all.* Because of the down-power risk that may be involved in telling an unpleasant truth and because people in up-power roles often feel immune to criticism, they are removed or remove themselves from the checks and balances of the feedback loop in which people tell each other either directly or indirectly about their impacts, both positive and negative. A healthy feedback loop is critical to positive working environments and good relationships.

A Few More Thoughts about Feedback

There is a popular saying: "Don't take anything personally," meaning don't take feedback personally. While this advice may save you from being hurt by negative criticisms and may reduce feedback anxiety, not taking feedback personally is actually an insult to a relationship. Although feedback is often a projection on the part of the giver, still there is almost always at least a little truth in what's been said. Not acknowledging this germ of truth demonstrates a lack of interest in and respect for the relationship. Lack of willingness to take feedback personally also robs you of the chance to use it to deepen and clarify the relationship. On the other hand, taking it ALL personally can make you an unwitting victim of the parts of the feedback that may be a projection and not have much to do with you at all. So we prefer to say, *Don't take ALL of it personally and don't not take NONE of it personally.* Or those of you familiar with the Twelve Step Program will recognize the suggestion given to participants in that context to "take what you like and leave the rest."

Amina Knowlan, a group-leadership trainer, offers these further insights: *"Conflict, in my experience, is often a hyper-charged backlog of undelivered feedback. By the time we deliver the feedback, there is such a build-up of dissatisfaction that it often comes with an intention and tone that sounds like a demand for change or even a threat. If I am giving you feedback about the impact of your behavior on me, I am not blaming you or making you responsible for that impact. I am offering data about your impact on me as a way of opening the communication between us and improving our relationship. If we understand feedback as an investment in relationship, how could we not want to receive feedback about our impact? Why would we spend so much time defending our intentions rather than just staying curious?"*

Appreciation and Kindness

Appreciation is a powerful form of feedback. While it may seem that people learn most from feedback about things they can or should change (negative feedback), positive feedback is really more powerful. One of Cedar's clients reported that she felt like she was always criticizing her husband and he was always feeling hurt and nagged. It was a recipe for a lot of pain. After exploring this issue in the session, she went home, told her husband how bad she felt about this, and asked him if he had any suggestions. He responded, *"Most of the things you are critical of I really want to change, for you and also for myself. But I feel mad and frustrated when you keep pointing out the same things. Here's what will work. Say it once. I'll check and see if it is something I want to change. Then don't mention it again. Instead, be on the lookout for when I do it right and let me know you've noticed and appreciate it. If it's something I don't want to change, then we have to have a different discussion."*

As this request shows, we seem ever ready for being hurt or criticized. Thus we long for kindness and affirmation. Good acts and kindness are contagious. A 2010 study by researchers from the University of California and Harvard found *"the first laboratory evidence that cooperative behavior is contagious and that it spreads from person to person. When people benefit from kindness, they 'pay it forward' by helping others who were not originally involved, and this creates a cascade of cooperation that influences dozens more in a social network"* (Inga Kiderra, "'Pay it Forward' Pays Off," www.ucsdnews.ucsd.edu, March 5, 2010). We remember a particular occasion when we paid the toll for the person behind us—a random stranger. That driver couldn't believe it, but we were pretty sure this gesture had made his day. It actually made ours too.

There's a program called *Appreciative Inquiry (AI)*. AI trainers begin every consultation by asking, "What's going well here?" In one of our practice exercises, we ask people to tell their partners what was most helpful to them or what worked best (of the things they did or said). Remarkable learning comes from appreciation. Research shows that a great predictor of successful marriages is the frequency with which the partners verbally appreciate each other. We've heard of a family that begins their Friday-night meal with appreciations. Some of the best teachers we know get great results by catching children doing a desirable behavior, like sharing or speaking up or being kind, and praising the "perpetrators." *"I noticed you were being very gentle with the cat. The cat likes that."* Give praise right away. Praise offered immediately has greater impact. And be as specific and accurate as you can. Try out the Appreciation Circle exercise in the **"Try This"** section of the book.

In conclusion, learn to live in the Power Zone by practicing not only the Golden Rule but also the Golden Mean. Moving appropriately back and forth within reasonable limits along different spectrums of behavior will prove the key to success in life, work, and love. It's a matter of balance and moderation as well as experience. And the best tool to help you find and stay in the Power Zone is without doubt learning to ask for, give, receive, and apply effective feedback, while thinking of it not as criticism but as an investment in relationship.

Chapter 5:

Strengthening Your Core

RIGHT USE OF POWER

CHAPTER 5:

Strengthening Your Core

A strong, resilient core is the foundation for living in the Power Zone. Attending to self-care is the best way to strengthen our core. In truth, we misuse power against ourselves when we don't take good care of ourselves.

How selfish that sounds! Isn't the whole emphasis of the Judeo-Christian tradition on putting others first? Perhaps. But non-swimmers can't be lifeguards, and poor people can't endow charities. So to use our power wisely and well, we have to include caring for ourselves.

Sitting with her seatbelt fastened on one of her many flights, Cedar suddenly understood something from the announcement she had half-heard dozens of times before: *"If there is a sudden decrease in cabin pressure, oxygen masks will automatically fall from a compartment above your head. Place the mask over your nose and mouth and breathe normally. If you are traveling with a small child or infant, please put your own mask on first before trying to assist others. . . ."*

Why do flight attendants say that? Well, at 40,000 feet the air is so thin that you have only about 30 seconds to start receiving emergency oxygen before you pass out. If you try to help someone else, you may not be able to get either of the masks on in time, and both of you will suffocate. On the other hand, if you attend to yourself first, you'll have the best chance of saving yourself and the other person too.

As it turns out, self-care is not selfish. Far from it! In fact, the lack of adequate self-care is a major factor in the misuse of power. Furthermore—and this may surprise many readers—failure to take care of ourselves is actually a misuse of power towards ourselves. And we are not just talking about getting too little sleep.

Reynold Ruslan, for example, suffers from hypertension. Fortunately, through maintaining his weight, exercising, and taking medication, he manages to keep his blood pressure in the normal range. Nonetheless it occasionally spikes, often in autumn with a sudden drop in temperature. By taking extra medication, he can usually get it back to normal in a day or two. Still, while it is high, he is not so pleasant to be around. He doesn't smile, has no energy, and is typically in a bad mood.

The point is it's hard to use your personal, positional, or status power well when you're out of sorts. Think of how you are as a boss or colleague after a night of poor sleep or when your arthritis or stomach is acting up or when you've been overworking for a week or more to get some project done or when the boss has been on your case. Nice as you may be when things are going well and you've been taking good care of yourself, you may not be so nice when they aren't and you don't. "What's wrong with Mom?" The kids ask their father in the evening. "Oh, she's just had a horrible day at the office. Why don't you kids go over to your friends' for a sleepover? Mom should be better after a good night's sleep."

And What about You?

Now imagine hearing the words *"It's okay to take care of yourself."* Do you stop yourself with one or more of the following "reasons"? Check all that apply to you.

- I don't have the time to exercise or play. ( )
- I need to work more to make it financially. ( )
- My mother always said, "Idleness is the Devil's workshop." ( )
- There are too many demands on me—work, relationships, children, finances—and I always seem to come last. ( )
- The only time I get to stop is when I'm sick. ( )
- Whenever I take time off, I have to work too hard to catch up. ( )
- I feel ashamed if I'm too needy, so I just stuff my feelings and soldier on. ( )
- I have a strong ethic of service. ( )
- When I get exhausted, I'm ashamed that I haven't taken care of myself and then feel even worse about things. ( )

Inadequate Self-Care Leads to Misuse of Power Towards Others.

Inadequate self-care is an ethical issue precisely because of the vicious cycle or downward spiral it creates as shown in the diagram below. When we are stressed, blood flows from our brain to our extremities to prepare us for fight or flight. As a result, we are less able to be connected and to deal creatively with challenges. *Note: the term* resourced *as used below means being connected with and supported by personal resources, e.g. centeredness, confidence, compassion, education and training, supervision, empowerment, and a social network.*

> **Lack of self-care contributes to stress, burnout, and dulled awareness.**

> **These conditions interfere with our normal abilities to feel resourced and to handle difficult situations.**

> **Being un-resourced increases our vulnerability to misusing our power.**

Signs of Inadequate Self-Care

How do we know when we have been neglecting ourselves? Mostly we are aware when we get stressed out. However, to fine-tune things, here are some indications that we not been attending adequately to our physical, mental, emotional, or spiritual needs. Once again, check those that currently apply to you. (Perhaps use a pencil and date your entries so that you can come back in future to see what progress you've made.)

- My judgment seems impaired. ( )
- I have difficulty being alert or attentive. ( )
- I am less warm or generous than usual. ( )

- I become increasingly defensive. ( )
- I get unusually moody. ( )
- I am more easily triggered by small disturbances—the dog barking, a child asking for help, etc. ( )
- I have too much or too little self-confidence. ( )
- My boundaries seem poorly defined. ( )
- I tend to get over- or under-involved in things. ( )
- I feel too much or too little compassion. ( )
- I am unusually resentful. ( )
- I get ill or burnt out. ( )
- I am sick frequently and have difficulty staying healthy. ( )

We Can Misuse Power Toward Ourselves.

Being attuned to our impact on others, we may forget that our behavior impacts us too. This situation occurs when we fail to

1   Prevent or reduce harm to ourselves;
2   Repair harm to ourselves; and/or
3   Promote our personal well-being.

Here are three stories that illustrate what we mean.

Story: **Preventing or reducing harm to ourselves.** *Angie was constantly critical of herself. In her eyes she was too messy, not kind enough, usually unprepared, and always late. Thinking that through self-blame she was helping herself become a better person, she was in fact disempowering herself by reducing her self-confidence and shaming herself. One day her therapist caught her in a moment of self-appreciation when Angie said, "You know, I handled that situation at work really well." Then she immediately began to disparage herself. Her therapist said, "Hey, let's take a moment to acknowledge that you've done something well. It's an important thing to do. Let's light a candle to celebrate your success." Angie began to cry. "I guess I've never learned to appreciate myself," she said. "The only thing I ever got acknowledged for as a kid was getting good grades."*

Story: **Repairing harm to ourselves.** *Angie took the candle home with her. Every evening she would light it and name something she had done well that day. As she later told her therapist, "I'm amazed at how helpful this little thing is. I am actually getting into the habit of feeling good about myself. I can't believe how much more confident I feel. It's like putting a Band-Aid of appreciation over old hurts to give them a chance to heal."*

Story: **Promoting personal well-being:** *In one of Cedar's sessions, she was upset with herself because she was over-tired and couldn't keep her eyes open. After valiantly fighting it for a while, she told her client, "I'm really sorry, but I'm feeling sleepy. This isn't about you. I'm going to take a short break to wake myself up." When Cedar came back, her client had teared up. "What you did really touched me. I can't tell you how many times I've been there trying not to fall asleep and feeling guilty. It never occurred to me that I could be honest and do something to wake up. I'm so relieved to know that you take care of yourself. And it wasn't a problem. In fact, while you were gone, I got in touch with something I wanted to talk about with you."*

Self-Care Is More than Getting a Good Night's Sleep.

There are many ways of taking care of ourselves. Here, are a few tips.

1   **Work:** Maintain an appropriate workload. Also, if you are stuck in a job you dislike, have the courage to look for something better or more in synch with your talents and interests. We spend most of our waking lives at work. So, if push comes to shove, we need to downsize our lifestyle to make more fulfilling but less well-paying work possible. No one wants an epitaph that reads, "Here lies_____ who spent her life doing work she hated. Fortunately she's free of that now";

2   **Diversity:** Create a diversity of expressive, recreational, and spiritual activities. The point is to find things that are fun or otherwise meaningful to do and do them on a regular basis. The most satisfying, stress-free life is one that's marbled with fun and meaningful activities outside of work. As Archbishop Desmond Tutu puts it, *We humans can tolerate suffering but we cannot*

tolerate meaninglessness (*God Has a Dream: A Vision of Hope for Our Time*, 2004, p. 75).

3 **Savor and Serve**: Develop the ability to savor as well as serve. The choice is not between one and the other. We need to find joy in service while doing service in the midst of life's pleasures.

4 **Prioritize Self-care:** Set a high priority on self-care. It's so easy to forget about going to the gym or taking a regular nap or just sitting on your deck and watching the scene outside. Take opportunities to goof off. Being happy and nourished is a basic self-care strategy that strengthens the core. Find novelty in your daily routine. Laugh! Laughter significantly reduces anxiety, lightens burdens, and shifts our perspective.

5 **Prioritize What's Most Important**: *Stephen Covey tells a great story (*First Things First*, 1996) tells a great story about priorities. He takes a big glass jar and fills it first with fist sized-rocks, then gravel, then sand, and finally water. Before adding each new thing to the jar, he asks the audience if the jar is full. First they say no and then they get the idea. After putting in the water, he asks them what the point of the story is. One person says, "The point is that no matter how full my schedule is, there is always room for one more thing." Nope, says the lecturer. The point is that if you don't put in the big rocks in your life first, you'll never be able to fit them in! Take a minute to notice what the big rocks in your life are.* (See also: www.dailyblogtips.com/put-the-big-rocks-first/)

6 **Limitations and Strengths:** Honesty is the best policy here. Ask for support in knowing both your limitations and your strengths and then use this information to help your collaborate. Don't expect to be able to do everything.

7 **Compassion for Others**: With good self-care you will be less likely to experience what we have come to call "compassion fatigue." Compassion fatigue is best described as what happens when, as the Buddhists put it, you get into the sinking ship with the person you are trying to help rather than tossing them a life-line. Joan Halifax gives us the lifeline point of view. *Compassion, as the capacity to be attentive to the experience of others, to wish the best for them, and to sense what will truly serve when we allow*

our natural impulse to care for another become a source of nourishment rather than depletion.

8 **Gratitude:** Research shows that gratitude has a powerful physiological and emotional effect. In a study in which people were given the assignment of simply listing every week five things they are grateful for, *those in the gratitude group felt better about their lives overall, were more optimistic about the future, and reported fewer health problems than the other participants.* Results were even better for those who named gratitudes as a daily practice. **Try it out.**

(For more on gratitude, see the article by Bruce Campbell at www.cfidsselfhelp.org/library/counting-your-blessings-how-gratitude-improves-your-health.)

Developing Resilience Is the Key to Strengthening Your Core.

Resilience is so important that we would like to speak of it in more detail. Simply put, resilience is the ability to bounce back—to cope successfully with adversity or risk and to learn new skills from doing so. Resilient people are like trees that can bend with the wind: they are strong yet flexible. Happily, you don't have to be born with resilience; it is something that can be learned. One helpful way is through using the Resilience Cycle. This is a set of four phases—*relaxation* (where we recharge), *clarity* (where we create a strategy), *effectiveness* (where we implement our ideas), and *satisfaction* (where we reflect on the whole process). All four phases are important. Repeated use of the Resilience Cycle tends to build or strengthen this capacity in us over time, and eventually its use becomes habitual.

In the process of moving around the Resilience Cycle, you may find places where you get stuck. These are called *barriers*—habits that interfere with satisfying and effective movement around the cycle. A habit like automatic confusion, for example, will interfere with getting clarity. This is an insight barrier. The inability to take action through delay or taking too many actions is called a response barrier. Habits of denying needs or not taking the time needed to integrate and appreciate success are called nourishment-barrier responses. Inability to complete and let go is called a completion barrier.

Omitting any phase can disturb the cycle.   Here are some examples.   Leaving out **clarity** leads to wasted action; **effectiveness,** frustration and emptiness; **satisfaction**, lack of pleasure, appreciation, and integration; **relaxation**, too little room for the next idea or need as well as the next round of the cycle.   Noticing your barrier habits and then letting go and reorienting can help you move more smoothly around the cycle.

Here's how the resilience cycle looks as a chart:

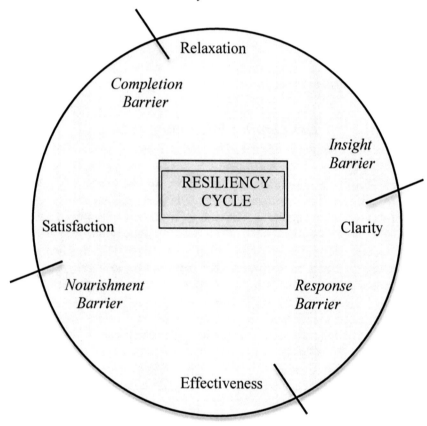

Another technique for being resilient is to take three deep breaths. Try it now and see how you feel afterward. This resource can be practiced whenever things start getting to you. You'll be surprised how quickly this simple technique will set you up again. Just three breaths can change your whole perspective. Never be too busy to take three breaths.

Time Can Be Your Friend.

The piano virtuoso Artur Rubenstein was once asked by an admirer, "How do you handle the notes as well as you do?" The maestro answered, "I handle the notes no better than many others, but the pauses—ah, that's where the art resides." Today we live in "microwave time" where everything needs to be done immediately. Imagine if there were no clocks, and time were organic. In Australian Aboriginal culture, the beginning of an activity is not set by the minute, the hour, or the day, but by when all the right people have shown up. Just as Rubinstein did, we can learn the art of the pause, for therein lies much of the art of living.

In our increasingly speeded-up world, empty space seems harder to come by and justify. Peter McDonald offers some good guidance for the relaxation phase of the resilience cycle: *"Between endings and beginnings there is a blank time where nothing is supposed to be this way. Like a tree in winter, on the outside there is nothing going on, but inside is hidden growth. The growth explodes in spring. Spring can't happen without the blank time."*

In fact, we can come to understand time like the gears on a bicycle. Just as there are different gears for different terrains, so we can shift the gears on how we use time. Unconsciously, most of us already know how to do this. Think about such things as responding to an emergency, listening to a friend who needs support, paying the bills, resolving a conflict, going through our new emails, meditating, being in nature, or doing a creative activity. The actual time spent on these things may be the same, but the experienced time will seem slower or faster, more or less intense, for each. Learn to up- or downshift according to the time needs of a task. The key, according to Stephan Rechtschaffen, is *"to be consciously awake and alive while sweeping the floor, driving a car, or walking along a city street, [in order] to expand the ordinary moment and make life more full."*

Track How You Are Doing.

The main thing is, as we argued in the last chapter, to attend to yourself first. Here are three questions to track how you are doing:

1   **Am I living wisely?**
2   **Am I loving well?**
3   **Am I contributing?**

Internet Technology

What a surprise! Technology, meant to save us time and effort, has opened up vast new worlds and possibilities that both astound and addict. In the last few years we have gained the ability to use our power to have an expanded effect through social-media marketing. We have the ability now to find, re-connect, and stay in touch with a huge number of friends, causes, and organizations through the Internet, Facebook, and Twitter. We can sit together in a restaurant and get an instant answer to any questions through Google.   We can make greatly enhanced presentations through PowerPoint. We could go on. Unfortunately, our sense of how best to relate to others in this new technological world has yet to be formed. Joseph Firmage (as adapted by Cedar Barstow) speaks of this revolution in its broadest context: "*The greatest revolutions science and technology have presented to us across history point to a fundamental revolution of the human spirit and ethic equally profound waiting in the wings.*" We are the ones who must activate this spirit and ethic.

We can help ourselves stay in the Power Zone in our high-tech world by first looking at the ways in which our relationships are off balance.

In this regard, here are a few questions to ask:

- Do I spend too much time on the Internet?
- Does my Internet usage have an addictive quality?
- Do I find my relationships through the Internet are shallower than my in-person relationships?
- Do I get overly hyped up?

- Do I feel duty bound to respond to emails immediately even when the subject may require time for processing and being creative?

If you answered *yes* to one or more of these questions, you'll need to find solutions to bring you back into a healthy balance. Here are several possibilities.

- Budget and then schedule your time on the Internet. Use a timer if that helps. When it goes off, stop even if you aren't done.
- Separate your emails into categories and deal with each separately.
- Because all emails look the same (same font and size), it's easy for them to seem equally important. Recognize this phenomenon as a kind of visual tyranny.
- Make sure to balance your in-person relationships with your virtual ones.

Our local daily, the Boulder *Daily Camera*, on Feb 10, 2013, reprinted an article by Joanna Weiss from the *Boston Globe* titled "Your Boring Facebook Friends." According to Ms. Weiss, some 67% of adult Americans use Facebook. However, a February 2013 survey by the Pew Internet & American Life Project found that 61% of the users *have taken a Facebook vacation "[because they were] too busy or just [weren't] interested [or felt] it [their usage] was a waste of time."* Lee Rainie, the director of the Pew project, concluded that *"people are [now] making little mental calculations about how much time [they] want to devote to this, [and] the quality . . . of the material [they] get from [their] friends."* So, according to the article, we may be beginning to find a less compulsive, more mature relationship with Internet technologies based on our need for self-care and real-time, higher-quality in-person relationships with our families and friends. Right use of electronic power is complex. As in all uses of power, the best is mixed with the worst, the vicious and the virtuous, and we are being challenged to find our way in a world of resources that gives us access to tremendous quantities of free information as well as annoys us with hacking and the difficulty of discerning the true from the false. Humanity hasn't dealt with these particular issues before. Applying an ethic of caring about and taking action for the common good is one helpful way through.

Support

Ralph Waldo Emerson, the 19th-Century sage of Boston, wrote, *"There is guidance for each of us, and by lowly listening we shall hear the right word. . . . Place yourself in the middle of the stream of power and wisdom that flows into your life. Then, without effort, you are impelled to truth and to perfect contentment."* He makes it sound so simple! Finding this guidance and support is a matter of going both inside to our intuition and outside to families, friends, and communities. The basic guidance may be there, but it is up to us to listen for it or search it out and then follow it.

Some years ago Cedar's brother Dave, the founder of EMPACT Africa whom we met in an earlier chapter, learned something important about support from his wife, Linda. She said, *"When I'm upset or complaining about something, sometimes I want sympathy and sometimes I want solutions. It will work best if you ask or, or better yet, if I tell you whether I need sympathy or solutions."* This is one way to be sure you get the kind of support you want and need. Another is to choose whom to confide in and with whom you can safely let your vulnerability show. There are some important qualities that make for a good support person: Are they emotionally available? Do they have the time? Are they compassionate? Do they have good boundaries? Will they be honest with me? Can they provide an outside perspective? Can they be encouraging? Will they keep what I tell them to themselves?

Empowering Yourself.

This chapter has been about strengthening your inner self, or core, so that you can live more consistently in the Power Zone. As you know, we all have power—the ability to have an effect and influence—and yet we seem to keep losing it and having to find it over and over again. As Alice Walker poignantly says, *"The most common way people give up their power is by thinking they don't have any."* We give it up when we've been hurt, when we equate down-power with no power, when we think we are at risk, and when we don't take good care of ourselves.

Story: Imagine what it would take to empower yourself as a prisoner. Here's a story written with understandable pride by a prisoner, and found in a newsletter written by and for prisoners. *Martin Luther King said, 'The true mark of growth isn't how a man acts when or during times of comfort and happiness, rather how he acts during times of trials and controversy.' I put that to the test last week. On my way to chow the Assistant Chief of Security pulled me aside and searched me. My shoes had a hole in the heel from daily wear. He accused me of using it as a hiding spot for contraband. He told me to go to my room and don't leave it until he came to pick them up. I didn't protest or complain. I didn't say a word the whole time. I came to my room. I sat in there until the next day. I missed breakfast, supper and my shower. When the Sergeant came to pick them up, didn't say nothing. I just handed them to her. When she asked what I wanted done with them, I said, 'Put them on the Chief's desk cause he wants them so bad.' That is the best behavior I ever displayed in a situation such as this.* Even when treated unjustly, this man is doing his inner work of remaining centered and strong.

(For more about the Prison Outreach Project founded by Anna Cox, see www.compassionworksforall.org)

On the other hand, we can express powerlessness by becoming overpowering. Jean Baker Miller describes this kind of out-of-the-zone misuse of power well: *"The need to control and dominate others is [often] psychologically a function not of a feeling of power but rather of . . . powerlessness. . . . The power of another person or group of people was generally seen as dangerous. You had to control them or they would control you. But in the real world of human development, this is not a valid formulation. Quite the reverse. In a basic sense, the greater the development of each individual, the more able, more effective, and less needy of limiting or restricting others she or he will be."* Using power wisely and well—which means having a balanced use of power, neither under- nor over-using it—is nourishing and effective. It evolves through a self-correcting process of losing your power, then finding it again. Each time you do will add more strength to your core.

Let's give the last word on the subject of this chapter to the poet Gary Snyder: *The power within—the more you give, the more you have to give—will be our source when coal and oil are long gone, and atoms are left to spin in peace.*

Chapter 6:

Resolving and Repairing Interpersonal Difficulties

RIGHT USE OF POWER

CHAPTER 6:

Resolving and Repairing Interpersonal Difficulties

A High Art and Skill

"I was thinking of a time when someone was venting blame towards me. I was able to breathe and stay calm and present, but I could feel the storm of emotion and words roll off me as I tried to stay connected in myself. I have much to learn about repair." [Leela] Resolving relationship difficulties is a high art and a complex skill. Indeed, peace-filled interpersonal and global relationships depend on ALL of us learning how to be peacemakers.

We've all been hurt. We've all caused hurt. Some hurts are intentional. Some are unintentional. All hurts deserve to be resolved and repaired. Resolution-and-repair comprises one of best uses of our power and influence.

Wounds caused by misuses or abuses of power too often end in the loss of a relationship and unhealed pain. As a result, many of us associate conflict itself with loss and pain. Given this association, it is hard for us to see conflict as offering opportunities for healing, relationship repair, and even the deepening of trust and connection. This possibility is, for many, a big surprise and a new way of responding to conflict.

Story: *A group Cedar was working with in Ireland had developed a conflict. Over the course of an hour or so, they successfully worked it out. She was proud of them and expected they would be light and happy the next morning. However, when she arrived in the meeting room, she was surprised to find many of them crying. It seems their experience of prior conflicts had been so consistently traumatic that they were unable to accept that their recent one had been so easily resolved. As Cedar talked with them, their pain turned to relief, and they ended the morning by feeling more connected with each other than before the conflict. They were crying now from happiness and relief, they said, because they had never experienced resolving conflict in this way before.*

The simplest and easiest way to resolve a difficulty is to attend to it as soon as possible. This point is obvious. It is nevertheless a challenging task because we must stay hopeful, compassionate, non-defensive, curious, and skilled throughout the process. That's a tall order.

Escalation of Conflict

When not handled right away, issues tend to escalate quickly. This is how it went in one situation. Story: *Steve, the teacher in a small interactive class, asked a student a question that elicited a very personal response. The student immediately felt ashamed of her disclosure and withdrew within. Steve didn't attend to her reaction. The student attempted to talk to Steve about it several times, but he didn't get it. Her shame deepened. She told her friends that this teacher was someone who shamed people. Word reached the head of Steve's Department. An ethics complaint was filed. Resolution was long and hard in coming. Like this student, most people make several attempts to let those up-power from them know when there's a problem. Unfortunately, the latter sometimes justify their actions to themselves and refuse to respond until things have spiraled out of control.*

Here's how escalation usually looks and the stages at which a problem can be resolved, albeit with increasing difficulty:

1. Simplest, most satisfying, and most effective is a personal conversation immediately after a difficulty has emerged.

2. Personal conversation at a later time can still work.

3. Sometimes a conversation with a third party present is useful.

4. A formally mediated resolution may forestall harder measures.

5. A grievance process or legal action is the final, least pleasant type of resolution.

We want to say that there are, of course, conflict situations in which trying to resolve the issue by either party alone is not advisable. Examples are when physical abuse, potential danger, and violent or explosive conditions are present. In these cases, contacting a supervisor, calling the police, getting out of harm's way, or working with a therapist would be more viable—and safer—solutions.

Unlinking Conflict from Unresolved Pain and Loss

Most people based on past experience have an often-unconscious expectation that any conflict will result in pain and loss, even trauma. To demonstrate and experiment with this expectation, we ask workshop participants to link their fingers to show the amount of connection they feel between conflict on the one hand (!) and hopelessness, loss, and pain on the other. (Tightly interlocked fingers indicate a strong connection, while fingers held more loosely and further apart show a lesser connection.) Then we invite the participants to try slowly to move their hands apart, symbolizing their unlinking the automatic bond between conflict and loss or pain. Working with her hands, Connie discovered that the amount and intensity of coupling depended on who was initiating the resolution process. Adam found his hands so tightly linked that it was difficult to choose to unlink them. **Try this** two-part exercise yourself. Naturally, actual unlinking in real life requires more attention than this one simple process. However, uncoupling this automatic connection opens psychological space in which it is easier to resolve and repair interpersonal difficulties.

Stages in Resolving Difficulties

Resolving relationship difficulties generally proceeds in the following stages.

1. Find your compassion, curiosity, and non-defensiveness.

Barbara Kingsolver says, "*Pain and sorrow, they are a mystery. Kindness and love, they are a mystery. But I have learned that kindness and love can pay for pain and sorrow.*" Compassion is the ability to feel another's suffering as both different from yours and yet connected to your own. Suffering is thus a universal experience. This fact can inspire us to get back in touch with a person we've hurt in order to resolve and repair the difficulty or misunderstanding. Resolving relationship difficulties is really an expression of care, integrity, and confidence rather than an action based on fear of punishment. Compassion accompanied by curiosity softens our hearts and refocuses the inquiry rather than inciting blame or judgment. Curiosity in fact builds connection and collaboration.

One of the simplest ways **to activate compassion** is by simply taking three deep, slow breaths. Another, as suggested in the "**Try This**" section of the book, is to recall a time when you were wounded by someone in authority. Then think about what the person didn't know that led them to hurt you. What curriculum would you design for that individual? Here are some thoughts from past workshop participants: *"He needed to learn respect for those down-power to him." "She needed a class in simply listening." "He needed the whole Right Use of Power program." "She was lashing out because she had so little self-esteem; so I'd suggest a self-esteem class." "Well, he needed an ethics class—not just to memorize the rules but to understand the dynamics." "She needed to understand the 150% Principle. With that one idea, everything would have been different."* This exercise of "creating a curriculum" can help us have empathy for others who have hurt us. But compassion need not stop here. We also misuse power by not having compassion for our own suffering and mistakes.

To activate your curiosity, try this: Either in your mind or facing a partner, imagine that you two have a conflict. Feel the gravity of this problem in the space between you. Now turn your backs to each other and change **only one** thing—engage your curiosity. Then face each other again and see what's different. Here are some responses we've heard in workshops: *"Remarkable! Now I'm focusing on my partner instead of the problem." "The problem doesn't seem so overwhelming now." "I suddenly have a little hope instead of just dread."*

To activate your non-defensiveness, start by remembering that in the complex world of relationships and power, the idea that you could "cause no harm," as in the Hippocratic Oath, is unrealistic and often creates a defensiveness which interferes with relationship repair. We cause harm even if we don't intend to. We make mistakes just because we're human. And people misunderstand us just because they are. Life's like that. So, rather than imagining that if we have good intentions no one will be harmed—and therefore if they do feel harmed, it was somehow their fault, not ours—we need to practice non-defensively tracking for trouble so that we can clear it up before it escalates.

Upsets, difficulties, and conflict are things we can learn from whichever side of the conflict we are on. The common saying "Don't take anything personally," as we mentioned earlier, is not completely helpful. When there is conflict, there is usually, although not always, a germ of truth for both sides to take in and consider. So we'd be helping ourselves and the situation by applying whatever is relevant and changing our behavior accordingly. This is the same idea we talked about in our discussion of feedback.

Another aspect of non-defensiveness is increasing our awareness of any habitual and dysfunctional conflict-avoiding strategies we may have. Since we have all been hurt by misuses of power, we have all developed protective conflict-avoiding habits.

Here are a few. Which ones do you identify with? Which ones do you recognize as strategies that others have used?

STRATEGY	MY HABIT	I SEE THIS IN OTHERS
over-analyzing		
shutting down and withdrawing		
shifting the blame		
taking all the blame		
minimizing or exaggerating a situation		
denying there is a problem		
defending good intentions		
ignoring the problem		
making a joke of the problem		
talking about it with others		
Other – note:		

2. Track for Trouble.

People let us know they are upset with something in a relationship in many ways. Their responses fall into three types of upset-indicators. Here we are building on the tracking and contacting skills we talked about in Chapter 3.

Expansive Indicators (which are expressive and easy to notice):
- direct statements of concern, fear, frustration, or anger
- bodily or facial signals of distress
- changes in breathing or eye contact, especially avoidance behavior

Contractive Indicators (which are less easy to notice and may seem unrelated to the issue):
- disguising a concern in a question
- disconnecting emotionally, withdrawing, or shutting down
- being late for a meeting or blowing it off

Internal Indicators (which are signs you notice in yourself):
- feeling triggered
- sensing that something is "off" in the relationship
- recognizing a familiar habit or avoidance reaction on our part.

3. Resolve and Repair the Difficulty.

Some conflicts are so painful or complex that they cannot be resolved within the relationship or right away. A severe or habitual abuse of power would be one example. Another would have to do with timing. In either an up- or down-power role, you may find that the other party is simply not available to respond. They may be too upset or have gone into fight, flight, or freeze behavior. In such a case it's best to wait till they are more available. Or the other person may simply, for whatever reasons, be completely unwilling to engage with you in resolving the situation. Then it's best to wait for a better time or move on.

However, based on personal experience and numerous studies, when the other party is willing, there are some simple things they need for resolution and repair. You may have identified some of them in remembering a time when you were wounded and what you would have needed from the other person for the situation to have turned out better.

So, shift your attention toward the difficulty with a stated intention of resolution. Be hopeful. Optimism like pessimism is often a self-fulfilling prophecy. Then trying out the suggestions in the chart below, see what's needed to resolve the conflict. The other party may need just the first thing (empathy), or they may require any or all of the additional pieces. Look for indicators that the situation has been resolved. You don't need to make a bigger deal of the conflict than it was or has become. Be sensitive to when you've done enough. Then stop.

Resolution and Repair from Up-power to Down-Power

What people need (any or all of the following):

1. ACKNOWLEDGEMENT
They want their experience acknowledged, understood, validated, and empathized with. They want to be appreciated for their courage in re-engaging with you.

2. UNDERSTANDING
They want to know what happened or what your intention was.

3. REGRET
They want a genuine apology or an authentic expression of your sorrow or regret.

4. LEARNING
They want reassurance that you've learned a lesson or understood something about yourself and how to care for them (and others) better in the future.

5. REPAIR
They want to reconnect with you and participate in repairing the relationship or in gaining clarity and letting go of their hurt feelings.

Two of these steps were a surprise to us. One was the generosity people feel when they understand (Step 4) that their pain or confusion may serve to prevent others from having a similar experience. As Marcus, one of our participants, said, *"It's easier to let this go because I know you learned something, and I believe you won't do this again."* It gives personal pain a larger meaning to know that it has served in some good way.

The other surprise for us was seeing how important it is for people who have become estranged to reconnect. *"Just your asking me what was needed for repair made me want to cry because I assumed you didn't care about me anymore."* Merely requesting to be reconciled after an inflicted hurt states an intention that can go a long way toward making things better. A successful resolution-and-repair process, moreover, usually results in increased trust, satisfaction, and health in a relationship. However, sometimes this process ends in a conscious decision to let go and move on. *"I got so clear that this was a relationship that wasn't going to work for me anymore. I've been in this place before, but this time it was a clear, conscious choice. It was sad, of course, but I don't have to drag the remnants along with me. What a relief!"* Or for Chuck, another workshop participant: "I *know I did my best. I know I gave it my all. It didn't get resolved. But I can now move on without always thinking that I should have done something else."*

In our workshops people are given just seven minutes to practice using these five reconciliation strategies to resolve a hypothetical conflict. Most are amazed at how far they are able to get in such a short time. We often think conflict resolution is a process requiring hours or even days. But in just seven minutes for each pairing most workshop dyads are able to complete the process in both directions or at least have gotten emotionally re-connected.

Of course, we grant that the "hurts" in our workshops are made up for the occasion. Real situations may take longer. But in our experience, using some or all of the five steps, above, can resolve even difficult situations in a lot shorter time than may have been initially supposed.

Resolution and Repair from Down-power to Up-power

The reconciliation process described here is especially useful for relationships in which the down-power person is the one distressed or confused, and the up-power person is initiating resolution and repair. This process provides the opportunity for up-power persons to employ the 150% Principle discussed earlier. It may even work between colleagues, friends, or partners, where there is no or little difference in power. But what about when a superior is misusing his or her power? There's always more risk involved when approaching a superior, or up-power individual, as we described in detail in Chapter 1.

It takes considerably more skill and care to be effective in resolving difficulties or addressing misuses of power with a superior. The power dynamics described in Chapter 1 typically affects the situation, often in ways we may not be aware of.

Here are two stories illustrating attempts at resolving a difficulty by a down-power person. One was successful, while the other was less so.

Story: *Jim's supervisor made it a practice to include the therapists he was mentoring in his groups as full participants along with the people they were seeing in private sessions as clients. Jim had spoken with his supervisor about his discomfort with this practice, but the supervisor did not change his approach. Jim talked with the other students and found they too were uncomfortable with the intended process. They decided that when all the group members were asked to pair up, Jim would state his professional discomfort and add that he would be role-playing in the exercise rather than being himself. His fellow students responded that they preferred to do the same thing for the same reason. Their plan was effective. By working together, they reduced the risk that one of them would be thrown out of the program. There was and is safety in numbers—a good example of* collective power. *By choosing another solution, they had enabled the supervisor to change the format without losing face.*

Story: *Sarah was a new teacher in a small private elementary school. The principal's policy was to keep the children inside when there was a strong wind on the playground. Sarah and the other teachers felt it was important for the children to go outside for exercise whenever possible. They noticed that the wind, earlier quite fierce, had died down. Sarah said she would call the principal and ask permission for the children to go out after all. The other teachers tried to dissuade her because of the principal's likely negative response. Sarah insisted, however, and did call the principal. "I know it was quite windy this morning, but now the wind has died down. Even the flag is still. I'm wondering if the children could go out for recess today. It's always good for them to get out." To everyone's surprise, the principal agreed. However, two days later Sarah was called into the principal's office. "I am dismissing you for challenging my authority, effective immediately. The other teachers will collect your things and bring them to you." Sarah had become the lightning rod for the principal's wrath and lost her job. She had been skillful in her feedback and was doing the right thing, but apparently the principal was too insecure in her authority or had too high a need for control. In any case, it's good to do the right thing, but it's always better to do so with skill and strategy and not to take too big a personal risk.*

We now offer you a few good ways to approach a person in an up-power role to resolve a situation. You will find a much longer list in the "Try This" section at the back of the book. Above all, be skillful and strategic, compassionate and courageous, and link a complaint with a specific request for change. As always, combine your power with compassion and understanding, for, as we say in our workshops, power with heart is the ultimate art.

We call this "down-power leadership." When Cedar asks an audience how many of them have had supervisors or employers who misused their power, everyone's hands go up! This is such an important topic that we will talk more about it in Chapter 8, which focuses on both up-power and down-power leadership.

4. Self-correct and Let go.

No matter what the outcome of your attempts to resolve and repair hurt feelings or a misunderstanding, it's useful to reflect on what took place. One helpful way is by asking yourself the following questions:

Self-correcting. What did you learn from this process—about yourself, about the other person, or about resolving and repairing a difficult situation? One of Cedar's teachers, Barney Aldrich, a master carpenter, once said, *"A good carpenter is not one who never makes mistakes, but one who knows how to fix them."* These wise words can help us achieve true mastery. An approach to reconciliation that includes personal growth not only leads to compassion in a relationship but is a major win/win technique in the art of living.

Letting Go. What do you need to let go? It might be expressing gratitude and relief that the process went well and the relationship is now repaired. Or it might be letting go when the attempt at reconciliation didn't end well, and it's clear that nothing more can be done. Or it might be noticing that there is an unhealed situation from the past that is still holding you back. Regarding the last case, you'll find a process for releasing a past situation that still haunts you in the **"Try This"** section.

Forgiving. Forgiveness is often misunderstood. It does not require forgetting or condoning an action. *"Forgiveness allows us to actually let go of the pain in the memory, and if we let go of the pain in the memory, we can have the memory, but it doesn't control us. When the memory controls us, we are then puppets of the past."* (Alexandra Asseilly, founder of the Forgiveness Project). Fred Luskin puts the point this way: *". . . Difficult things happen in life, and first you have to grieve them, then accept them, and finally move on. . . . Forgiveness means that unkindness stops with you. . . . This is not a one-time response. . . . It's about becoming a forgiving person."*

In the largest context, forgiveness has the power to stop the cycles of revenge and violence that drive egregious abuses of power. Luskin adds, *"By choosing to forgive, we stand in awe of the horrors that can happen to people in this world[,] and we decide neither to participate in them nor to repay them. It's not a matter of whether or not we will have conflict; it's a matter of what we do with that conflict."* Forgiveness can be a profoundly moving healing act that requires a lot of inner work in dealing with the grief and anger. We recommend an excellent film that shows the power of forgiveness in the lives of traumatically wounded people including: a daughter and the man who killed her father in Ireland, and a countrywide reconciliation process in Rwanda (Lekha Singh, *Beyond Right & Wrong: Stories of Justice and Forgiveness*, 2012, www.beyondrightandwrongthemovie.org).

To review: here is a schematic illustration of the four stages of the Resolving-Difficulties Process.

**4. Self-correct
and let go.**

**3. Stay
connected,
resolve and
repair things.**

*Resolving
Difficulties:
a process*

**1. Activate
compassion,
curiosity, and non-
defensiveness.**

**2. Track for
trouble.**

Chapter 7:

Overcoming Barriers to Power

RIGHT USE OF POWER

CHAPTER 7:

Overcoming Barriers to Power

The Mystery of Human Harm

Why do people cause harm? Abraham Lincoln is remembered as saying, *"Nearly all men can stand adversity, but if you want to test a man's character, give him power."* Indeed, power, the ability to have an effect or influence, is the ultimate test of not just character, but of one's ability to prevent and heal harm. Living in the Power Zone is thus another way to say acting ethically.

Cedar has wanted to answer the question of why people cause harm since she was an eight-year-old going to over-night camp for the first time. One of the girls in her tent had stolen comic books from another girl. According to Cedar's camp counselor, she became quit distressed over this misdemeanor and couldn't see why any child would want to steal.

As a mature adult, she came to understand a bit more about the dynamics involved when one has additional role or status power.

Story: *Henry Ford was born into a Midwestern farm family. He had an early interest in mechanics that his father noticed and supported. When Henry went to the city (Detroit) to get a job more connected with his talents than working on the farm, he was motivated to help the common worker. He wanted to create a car that would be affordable by everyone. Later, when Ford Motors already existed and Henry had built the wildly popular Model T, he doubled his workers' wages to $5.00 a day, a huge amount at the time. He knew the importance of a stable workforce. He also cared about his employees' housing and welfare. Once he amassed great power financially, socially, and organizationally, however, something changed. His workers seemed to become cogs in the wheel of his business success, he ruled his factory with an iron hand, he fought the labor unions, and he bullied his son, Edsel.*

This is not an unfamiliar story.   What happened?   Why is increased power so often a test that so many of us fail?

Here are some more examples. A department head was coercive; by shaming employees he created an unhappy, dysfunctional team. Even when given feedback about his negative impact, he insisted his was the only way to get things done. A doctor thought he was being a good listener for a patient's troubled home life. Soon he began confiding his own troubles, and before long he and the patient were having an affair. A father was mean to his son because the father was unhappy in his marriage. A spiritual leader had sex with women devotees for many years before the truth came out. He did what he did because, as he later put it, "It was good for them spiritually, and I could get away with it."

So, there are many reasons why someone with power would act unethically. Here are a few: naiveté, misunderstanding of the impact of the power differential, a forceful and controlling concept of leadership, not knowing the appropriate ethical guidelines, lack of skill, relational insensitivity, shame, self-protection, misplaced needs, poor judgment, and, like the guru just mentioned, thinking you can get away with it. Nowadays we don't advance "demon possession" as a likely cause for anything. Still, some individuals may simply have an evil turn of mind—What Herman Melville referred to as "motiveless malignancy."

But why then do we act ethically?   An evolutionary approach suggests that human beings are born with three nervous systems that have evolved over time.   When faced with a threat to survival, the most primitive response kicks in: we freeze. In animals this behavior is called "playing dead." In human being beings it looks like shutting down or withdrawing. For a mammal this reaction occurs when it experiences a life-threatening situation without the possibility of escape. The extremities go limp, and the life force seems to ebb away.

When a mammal perceives a lesser threat, it either runs or fights. This well-known fight-or-flee response is triggered by physiological activation of the muscles in the extremities. Then the animal or person either attempts to run away or fight its way out. This is the second level of nervous-system activation.

Researchers have now identified a third level for mammals they call the "social-engagement" nervous system (Steven Porges). This, the most recently developed in terms of Evolution, is the nervous system we use when we are concerned but still able to engage and are not overwhelmed with fear. It is also the one we use in everyday interactions with others. Unlike the earlier two, the social-engagement nervous system allows us to stay in relationship with others so that we can still collaborate while working out our differences.

Empathy, altruism, and socially engaged responses are supported by research on what are called "mirror neurons." These nano-particles were first noticed by accident in 1996 by Giacomo Rizzolatti and his team of researchers. When a graduate student eating an ice-cream cone returned to the lab, one of the researchers was amazed to see that the cells required to move food to a subject monkey's mouth and cause it to eat had fired without the monkey's hand and mouth having moved. (The monkey was hooked up to an EEG at the time.) The only stimulus appeared to be the monkey's observation of the student eating the ice cream. In follow-up research it turned out that *"humans . . . have mirror neurons that are far smarter, more flexible, and more highly evolved than any of those found in monkeys"* (Blakeslee, 2006). Remarkably, our brains light up in correspondence with someone else's activities and feelings if we are focused on that person. For example, when we see someone else in trouble, we automatically begin to feel concern about their well-being.

Neurological research by Moll and Grafman, moreover, has shown that taking action in the best interests of others is coded in our brains. In a study in which they scanned the *"brains of volunteers as they were asked to think about a scenario involving either donation of a sum of money to charity or keeping it for themselves,"* the results showed that *"when the volunteers placed the interests of others before their own, this feeling of generosity activated a primitive part of their brain that usually lights up in response to food or sex. Altruism, the experiment suggested, was not a superior moral faculty that suppresses basic selfish urges but rather a trait "basic to the brain, hard-wired and pleasurable"* (as quoted in Vedantam, 2007).

In an interesting study on babies and morality, toddlers were shown a scene in which a green puppet was trying to get a toy out of a box. Another puppet came along and closed the box to keep the puppet from getting the toy. Then a third puppet opened the box and helped the green puppet get the toy. Measured by their eye movements, the amount of attention paid, and their gestures, the young subjects preferred the kind puppet. After the show when they were offered a treat by both puppets, virtually all the toddlers preferred to take theirs from the helpful puppet. So, there seems to be a survival-related inborn impulse in us to use our capacities for empathy and social intelligence and for preferring the nicer person(s) in our environment. (See www.smithsonianmag.com/science-nature/Are-Babies-Born-Good-183837741.html.)

Cross-culturally there is agreement on the importance of honesty, responsibility, respect, and fairness in society (Kidder, 1994). This global agreement finds expression in the U.N. Universal Declaration of Human Rights, ratified in 1948. The very first article states, *"All human beings are born free and equal in dignity and rights. They are endowed with reason and conscience and should act towards one another in a spirit of brotherhood."* Spiritually there is also agreement about the value of an ethic of compassion: *"The early prophets did not preach the discipline of empathy because it sounded edifying, but because experience showed that it worked. They discovered that greed and selfishness were the cause of our personal misery. When we gave them up, we were happier. Egotism imprisoned us in an inferior version of ourselves and impeded our enlightenment"* (Armstrong, 2005).

Jonathan Haidt (as quoted in Goleman, 2008) named five moral rules found in most cultures:

> • *Prevent physical harm, protect the vulnerable, and restrain our violent impulses and those of others.*
> • *Do unto others what you would have them done unto you—the principle of moral reciprocity, AKA the Golden Rule.*
> • *Respect legitimate authority by deferring to those who hold social power and protect those who are dependent.*
> • *Be loyal by protecting the interests of our family or the groups we identify with most strongly, and*
> • *Respect sanctity by following the rituals and rules for right living we share with others in our group.*

Now, let's return to our initial question: Why do some people do terrible things to other human beings? If we have a social-engagement nervous system, mirror neurons, and altruism hard-wired to our pleasure centers as well as a global agreement on the basic values and moral rules regardless of religion or lack thereof, why do we cause harm? What are the barriers to the better uses of our power? What interferes?

The Barriers

Here are some.

- shame;
- the power paradox;
- unmet or misplaced ego needs including greed and an overweening desire for control, respect, power, money, sex, and/or affection (See the end of this chapter.);
- misinformation;
- lack of understanding of the impact of the power differential;
- past hurts, current pain, or habitual hurtful behaviors;
- a forceful, manipulative, controlling, or exploitive concept of power;
- an unwillingness to abide by ethical guidelines;
- stress and burn-out;
- an inability to be empathic;
- a lack of relational and communication skills;
- a strong need for self-protection;
- poor judgment;
- a desire for revenge; and/or
- obedience to directives from up-power person(s) or system.

Now let's talk a little more about two of the biggest barriers to using our power well: shame and the Power Paradox.

Shame

"Shame on you!" It's an expression we have all heard many times as we were growing up. The intention was to stop us from doing something grown-ups, typically our parents, considered inappropriate. If it worked, it might not only cut short our current misbehaving but keep us from acting out in similar ways in future.

So what's the issue here? The common understanding is that shame is one of the most effective ways to get people to behave well. Naturally, it should then be one of the most effective right-use-of-power tools we have. Yet the reality is that shame is such an intense and overwhelming emotion that people have a hard time recovering from it. In fact, they go to great lengths to avoid it. In naming and exploring the feeling of shame for the first time, one of our workshop participants said, "*I'm not kidding. This is real! This is not a role-play. This is how I feel all the time. I never had a name for it before.*"

Paradoxically, shaming ourselves out of doing something is just as likely to have the opposite effect. We may come to consider that we are unable to change—that this is just how we are. We act out because we are somehow innately naughty boys or girls. So rather than being shamed into "good" behavior, we are confirmed into bad.

Shame Keeps Us from Correcting Our Mistakes.

Here's how shame works. It's an attack on our core self which leaves us feeling guilty, incompetent, and worthy of blame because of an irreparable flaw, inadequacy, or our sinful nature. In other words, it reduces or even eliminates the possibility of self-correction or repair of harm in a relationship. Moreover, the everyday feelings of shame we endure have another downside: They take away the joy of living. Shame is such a terrible feeling of irreparable badness that we certainly don't want anyone else to know. It becomes our secret companion, always pulling us down and reminding us of our unworthiness. As it happens, we each feel shame from time to time and that feeling is quite similar—and similarly negative—for all of us.

Shame and Our Nervous System

Our nervous system responds to social stimuli in three ways: (1) as a kind of natural give-and-take; (2) as an invitation to fight or flight; or, most extremely, (3) as something which causes us, like a deer in the headlights, to freeze. When someone experiences shame, they usually freeze. They perceive it as a threat to themselves and their ability to survive. In this state, it is impossible for them to connect with others or to access inner resources to return to their ordinary self. As a result, they are traumatized. As with extreme fear or anxiety, shame disables the individual's ability to cope in normal social situations. Instead, their social-engagement nervous system is rendered inoperable.

Shame in Western Civilization

Here's a little history. According to Dutch historian John Huizinga (d. 1945), shame was used to keep Medieval Europeans from extreme behaviors. Huizinga found that *"the average European town dweller was wildly erratic and inconsistent, murderously violent when enraged, easily plunged into guilt, tears and pleas for forgiveness, and bursting with physical and psychological eccentricities"* (*The Waning of the Middle Ages*, 1919). Although positive reinforcement by addressing an individual's empathy, altruism, spirituality, or social responsibility is a more common approach today, many law suits, prisons, interrogation processes, parenting techniques, and educational methods still rely on shaming for behavior control.

Try this: Briefly remember a time when you felt shame, not an overwhelming shame, but one that you can learn from. This exercise will help you better understand this emotion.

Here are some of the effects of shame that others have named. Which ones do you recognize?

- gazing down or averting one's eyes,
- a sense of bodily collapse and compression,
- a feeling of heat or cold,
- shallow breathing,
- extreme intensity of emotions,
- a wish to die or disappear,
- an inability to connect,
- a loss of self-esteem, self-respect, or confidence,
- obsessiveness about something that has happened,
- a loss of internal resources, and/or
- rage focused either toward oneself or others.

The most potent of these effects are

- Isolation—lacking the desire or ability to connect with others;
- Loss of Inner Resources—feeling unable to access normal social skills and abilities like communication, problem-solving, and self-soothing;

- Hopelessness—believing we are irreparably bad and thus unable to recover; and
- Inability to Reality Check—being unable to discern the objective truth of a situation, like a rape victim who believes the rape was her fault.

Escaping the Shame Dungeon

Fortunately, there is a way out of what we call the Shame Dungeon. You don't have to feel good to do these things. You just have to do them, and little by little your sense of self will re-emerge:

- Move your arms and legs.
- Take deep breaths.
- Move your head from side to side.
- Sense your feet on the ground (and the ground under your feet).
- Stretch you limbs and facial muscles.
- Smile.
- Hum, sing, and make nonsense sounds.
- Laugh.

The last activity on the way out of this horrible prison is to reconnect with other(s) through eye contact. Here are what some of our workshop participants have said about this technique: *"When I got to the part about eye contact, I just couldn't open my eyes. Not for a while. When it felt safe and I felt big enough and myself again, then I could, and it felt so good." "Hey, you can't, you really can't feel shame at the same time as you are looking at someone else!" "Coming out of shame was an act of will, but I did it. It took wings of faith."*

Once out of the Shame Dungeon, you can feel support and are able to know whether you are the abuser or the abused. Then you can take action for healing.

If you are the **one who was harmed**, you will need

- a safe place to express anger, blame, resentment, or betrayal,
- an opportunity to grieve,
- a restored sense of self-respect and empowerment,

- openness to receive reparation and/or an apology,
- when the time is right, a courageous willingness to forgive, and
- a desire to let go, heal, and move on.

If you are the one **who caused harm**, you will need

- a safe place to express remorse, guilt, regret, or sorrow,
- an opportunity to deal successfully with the underlying issue(s),
- a restored sense of self-respect and self-worth,
- an openness to self-correction and to offering reparation to the injured party,
- forgiveness, if available, from that person, and
- a regained ability to be connected, heal, grow, and move on.

Shame is included in this section about overcoming our power barriers because it is often at the core of harmful, even extremely harmful behavior. Here's a simplified four-step process for de-activating your shame and helping others with theirs. Consider the following brief schematic, your GPS to get out of the Shame Dungeon.

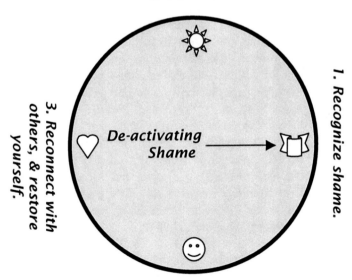

4. Let go, grow, & move on.

2. De-activate it using physical activities.

The Power Paradox

The Power Paradox is a surprising barrier to right uses of power. It typically affects people in up-power positions as a result of their being given more power than their ego can handle. Henry Ford's change of behavior, mentioned earlier, is an example of the Power Paradox in action. Named by Dr. Dacher Keltner, a professor of Psychology at the University of California, the Power-Paradox theory is supported by revealing studies as well as ubiquitous examples. In Dr. Keltner's words, *"Power is wielded most effectively when it's used responsibly, by people who are attuned to and engaged with the needs and interests of others. Years of research suggest that empathy and social intelligence are vastly more important to acquiring and exercising power than are force, deception, or terror. [However,] studies also show that once people assume positions of power, they're likely to act more selfishly, impulsively, and aggressively, and they have a harder time seeing the world from other people's points of view. This presents us with the paradox of power: The skills most important to obtaining power and leading effectively are the very skills that deteriorate once we have power."*

To put this idea another way, it seems that those who cultivate and use social intelligence, meaning modesty, empathy, engagement with the needs of others, and skill in negotiating conflicts, enforcing norms, and allocating resources fairly, are the ones who earn or are chosen for up-power positions. However, the research on the other side of the Power Paradox shows that *"power leads people to act in impulsive fashion, both good and bad, and to fail to understand other people's feelings and desires. . . . For instance, studies have found that people given power in experiments are more likely to rely on stereotypes when judging others, and they pay less attention to the characteristics that define those other people as individuals. Predisposed to stereotype, they also judge others' attitudes, interests, and needs less accurately. . . . Power encourages individuals to act on their own whims, desires, and impulses. . . . Perhaps more unsettling is the wealth of evidence that having power makes people more likely to . . . interrupt others, to speak out of turn, and to fail to look at others who are speaking"* (Keltner, 2008).

Here is a prime example. Sir Hari Singh (died in 1961), the last ruling Maharaja of the princely state of Jammu and Kashmir in India, was described by his son, Karan, as "a bad loser. Any small setback . . . would throw him in[to] a dark mood which lasted for days. And this would inevitably lead to what became known as a *muqaddama*, a long inquiry into the alleged inefficiency or misbehavior of some hapless young member of the staff or a servant. . . . *Here was authority without generosity; power without compassion"* (quoted by Tariq Ali in *The Clash of Fundamentalisms: Crusades, Jihads and Modernity*, 2002; italics added).

What factors would begin to explain this odd paradox? Consider these:

1) Because of the impact of the power differential, those in power-up roles are removed and remove themselves from the checks and balances of the feedback loop in which people tell each other either directly or indirectly about their impact, both positive and negative. When individuals are in power-down positions, as we've said, it may be too risky to offer negative feedback. The power-up persons too often seem to lose their perspective and over-react.

2) People tend to over-identify with their power role, experiencing their enhanced power as personal rather than role power. This misperception frequently leads to grandiosity and an unrealistic sense of self.

3) When in up-power positions, many individuals believe that the ordinary rules don't apply to them. Since they already have power, they don't think they are at risk of losing it—an unrealistic belief which keeps them from moderating overweening behavior.

4) Often, individuals lose empathy for those below them in the scheme of things.

5) Up-power individuals are also embedded in systems where it is difficult to act alone. One thinks of U.S. House Speaker Boehner, who on various occasions seemed on the verge of cutting a deal with the White House when his caucus forced him to back down. Even up-power people are not totally free in complex systems to do what they believe is right.

6) We have socially conditioned expectations and misconceptions about the use of power. We have long been accustomed to coupling it in our minds with manipulation, the undue use of force, coercion, terror, and deception. And so we acquiesce to this model even when it causes obvious harm to all concerned.

The Power Paradox, to be sure, doesn't affect every leader. Positive examples from recent history might include the likes of Nelson Mandela, Jimmy Carter, Mother Theresa, Mahatma Gandhi, the Dalai Lama, Hillary Clinton, and Bill and Melinda Gates. A lesser-known model for using power wisely and well is the current President of Uruguay, Jose Mujica. Elected in 2010, he chose not to live in the presidential palace but instead stayed close to his people in his modest village home. He would even make tea personally for his guests. According to him, *"It is not the man who has little but the man who craves more who is poor."* *Under his administration Uruguay "has enacted one of the region's most sweeping abortion rights laws [unusual in a Catholic country] and sharply boosted the use of renewable energy sources like wind and biomass"* (Simon Romero, "After Years in Solitary, an Austere Life as Uruguay's President," *New York Times*, January 4, 2013).

Similarly, some CEOs limit the amount of money they can earn by agreeing not to make more than four or five times the salary of their lowest paid full-time worker. Unfortunately, many more chief executives have no compunction about earning a hundred times more in addition to stock options and many other pricy perks. The latter individuals help us remember Lord Acton's famous saying that "power corrupts, and absolute power tends to corrupt absolutely."

It is thus important to immunize ourselves against using our power, especially role power, in life-denying, oppressive ways. In so doing we will be contributing to a new model of power we are calling the Empowerment Model. This is living in the Power Zone where power is used with compassion and strength to prevent and repair harm and to promote well-being and the common good.

Power Challenges

Right use of our power to prevent harm requires us to become more and more pro-active. Ethical pro-activity is connected to the Precautionary Principle, originating in Germany in the 1930s and now an important consideration for sustainable development and timely responses to global warming issues. This principle states that because of scientific uncertainty and the likelihood of harm, we must take precautionary action **before** we encounter danger rather than waiting for harm to happen (wikipedia.org/wiki/Precautionary_principle). Using the Precautionary Principle is an aspect of living in the Power Zone.

In becoming more and more pro-active, we need to get to know ourselves well and understand our impact in relationships and systems. This understanding helps us consciously avoid mistakes we might be particularly prone to make because of personal wounds, blind spots, habitual responses, naiveté, fear, or shame. As self-compassionate people, we need to remember that under certain circumstances, we are all capable of misusing, even abusing, our personal, positional, status, and collective powers.

Having read this far, you already know something about your own history and vulnerabilities, golden threads, and habitual responses. Here is another way in which you can practice pro-activity: to do your best to think ahead to what impacts your actions are likely to have. You may not be able to think as far ahead as seven generations, as American Indians suggest, but even one or two generations is helpful.

This next list may help you think about some potential blind spots in your uses of power. These are unmet needs you may unconsciously try to meet in ways that cause unintended harm.

- Do you have strong unmet financial needs?
- Do you have significant unmet social needs?
- Do you have deep unmet intimacy needs?
- Do you have an overwhelming need for approval?
- Do you have an overly strong need to be liked?
- Must you always feel that you are right?
- Do you have a pressing need to be in control?

All these are obviously normal human concerns. However, when they are overly strong or unmet, they can wreak havoc in our power relationships. For example, if we have significant unmet financial needs, we may be tempted to misuse our power by overcharging a client or cheating on our income taxes. If we have unmet intimacy needs, we may be tempted to seek an inappropriate and harmful sexual liaison with someone down-power from us. When we have too strong a need to be liked, we may under-use our power and not take charge when taking charge is needed. Under-use of power also causes subtle and unintended kinds of harm. If we must be in control in all cases, we may micromanage or bully our employees. Finally, if we have an overwhelming need to be right, we may act defensively, talk over others, or disregard their ideas even when they are good.

We wish you well in learning about the shadow aspects of your use of power and becoming more pro-active.   Preventing harm is easier and less stressful than resolving and repairing harm.

Chapter 8:

Leading Wisely and Well

RIGHT USE OF POWER

CHAPTER 8:

Leading Wisely and Well

Leadership of Self and Others

Leadership is the ability to use power effectively with oneself or others to achieve a goal. Self-leadership requires the individual to marshal his or her talents and strengths to get something done. Group-leadership is applying this skillset with others, be it in a business, the military, government, sports, or elsewhere. The latter is the more common understanding of the term. However, both definitions are correct.

Right use of power in a leadership role is based on preventing, healing, or repairing interpersonal harm, while promoting well-being and the common good. This is clearly a taller, more challenging order than simply achieving a goal. Goal achievement is a *what*; using power wisely and well is a *how*. Good leadership requires both. Right use of power is thus a matter of leaders being in right relationship with those who are down-power from them as they all work together to achieve shared goals. As Dacher Keltner says in an article in *Greater Good* magazine (vol. IV, no. 3), *"Power is not something we should (or can) avoid, nor is it something that necessarily involves domination and submission. We are negotiating power every waking instance of our social lives. . . . When we see equality, we are seeing an effective balance of power, not the absence of power. We use it [as leaders] to win consent and social cohesion, not just compliance. To be human is to be immersed in power dynamics."*

When Reynold Ruslan thinks of leadership, he envisions the conductor of a symphony orchestra. Although the members are undoubtedly capable as professional musicians of playing their parts well, the conductor has the role of interpreting the score and making sure through gestures and body language that his "forces" collectively perform the piece just as she or he has understood it. This means at different times speeding things up or slowing them down, bringing out one group of instruments while quieting others, indicating to a featured player when to enter or exit, and so on. Similarly, a former choir director of ours once said it was his job to make sure we all sounded like a single voice when we sang. In both examples, leadership is a kind of *e-pluribus-unum* (out of many, one) activity, to borrow the motto of the United States: creating from many parts a single, integrated whole.

A word of caution, though. Even the best leadership doesn't usually achieve perfection. It's important to keep our expectations realistic. Excellent presidential leadership, for example, won't lead to the fulfillment of every campaign promise. Assessing leadership fairly is a matter of discerning what a leader has been able to achieve in a given set of circumstances.

Not All Leaders Are Charismatic, and Not All Charismatic Leaders Are Good.

When people think of leaders, their image is often of individuals who are charismatic. However, not all leaders are charismatic, and not all charismatic leaders are good.

Although leadership is similar in *what* it does, the *how* is where the differences come in. Consider the following story: *As a manager, Lisa was near the top of her game. She was being considered for a position as a trainer in a corporate leadership program. After teaching a demonstration class, she received mainly positive feedback. One man, however, had this to say: "I'm sorry but you just don't have enough charisma. In my experience, this isn't something you can learn. You either have it or you don't." His opinion carried the day. Lisa didn't get the job.*

What is charisma? Leaders with this mysterious quality tend to have immense charm as well as outgoing, infectious personalities. Inspiring admiration when they speak, they generally hold their audiences in the palm of their hand. This, as in the story, is the prevailing notion of leadership.

Yet the downside of this kind of leadership is that it can inspire dislike as well as admiration. (Think of the American politician Newt Gingrich.) Charismatic leaders also tend not to collaborate very well and are usually defensive when they receive negative feedback. In this regard, the long-time Turkish Prime Minister, Recep Tayyip Erdogan, who is considered quite charismatic, is also known to be thin-skinned when it comes to criticism. It normally takes a large ego to be charismatic. Large egos are easily bruised. But getting back to Lisa, *she concluded that since a lot of charisma was needed for the training position, it wouldn't have been a good situation for her. Fortunately, she learned there are other effective leadership styles. Her confidence subsequently increased, and she eventually found a job that was a better fit for her personality.*

Four Types of Leaders

So, what about leadership styles, plural? In her research on power and leadership, Cedar concluded that just as power has many aspects and manifestations, the same is true for leadership. She eventually identified four basic styles. Power in each can be used poorly or well.

1. Leading from Information

This type is the leader as teacher—the teacher-in-chief, so to speak. This leader's focus is on presenting understandable information, citing theory, attending to details, being clear about boundaries, aiming for accuracy, and creating safety and trust with his/her followers through clarity. This kind of leader plans well in order to be prepared when interacting with his or her followers, team, or students. He or she tracks carefully to make sure the employees, troops, students, or clients understand the information being presented. This checking is often undertaken through frequent questions, requests for examples or applications, or—in the case of classrooms—quizzes and tests.

The downside of Informational Leadership is that it can be dry as well as out of touch with the feelings and lives of students or employees. It can also come across as all head and no heart. The chief architect of the U.S. involvement in the Vietnam War, Secretary of Defense William McNamara, was often accused of being a heartless technocrat who was more interested in numbers than lives. As the head of Ford Motor Company, before entering Government work, McNamara had a reputation for basing all his decisions on "the numbers." Later in life, though, he showed both compassion and remorse when admitting his grievous errors of judgment in Vietnam as documented in the film *The Fog of War*. Scientists like Albert Einstein and Niels Bohr are other examples of informational leaders as well as the physicist chancellor of Germany, Dr. Angela Merkel.

2. Leading from Self

This type is the Charismatic Leader. The focus here is on being centered, lively, and engaging; using one's personality to draw people in; sharing stories, insights, and jokes; being warm and congenial; encouraging risk-taking and self-reflection; and creating safety through their strength and persuasiveness. These leaders track how well their team, troops, or students are embodying what is being presented and how personally engaged with it they are. As mentioned above, the downside of charismatic leadership can be egotism, lack of collaboration, and unresponsiveness to constructive feedback, which such leaders tend to take as personal criticism.

Since this type corresponds in the popular imagination with leadership per se, there are many well-known examples. Among them are Bill Clinton, Billy Graham, Martin Luther King, and Archbishop Desmond Tutu.

3. Leading from Connectedness

We might call this type the Relational Leader. The focus for these individuals is on being in right relationship with their followers, making and sustaining healthy connections, encouraging active participation, resolving difficulties in the moment, and creating safety through an emotionally interactive environment. Tracking here consists of assessing from time to time how well the employees, team members, troops, or students are relating to both the leader and each other. The downside of this leadership style is that practitioners may get so involved in relationship dynamics (what we call the *how*) that they don't complete tasks (the *what*). Moreover, just because these leaders are more interested in the functioning of the team than their own role, we tend not to hear about them. Still, here are a few exemplars. Jim Sinegal, the co-founder and CEO of Costco, who is known for his modesty, participatory sense, and desire to treat all his employees, customers, and the larger community well would be one. The late Mr. Rogers of Children's Television fame is another possibility, and we suggest that Hillary Rodham Clinton with her team of loyal long-time helpers (known collectively as "Hillaryland") is a shining example.

4. Leading from the Whole

This type is the Visionary Leader. The focus here is on helping followers see and understand the full context of things, being flexible and spontaneous because everything relates to everything else, attending to flow and pacing, and creating understanding and a sense of safety through integrating information into a unifying theory or myth. The downside of this type of leader is the tendency to get too far ahead of his/her followers, become too theoretical, abandon practicality, and lose the attention and commitment of those following. Examples of this type of leadership are Mahatma Gandhi, Jean Houston, former U.S. Vice President Al Gore, and the late Steve Jobs.

What Kind of Leader Are You?

In truth, the best leaders have some skills from all four leadership types. But all of us have a style that feels easiest or most native to us. Now stop reading for a moment and reflect. Which of the above leadership styles feels most comfortable for you? Pick out one or two. Then consider strengthening these styles in both your personal and professional life. Next, choose one style that is not especially comfortable or natural for you. Then think of things you could do to increase your facility and skill in this area. Since it is unlikely that any of us will be equally proficient in all the leadership styles, it is helpful and relieving to accept and accommodate for those leadership types that we have less of an affinity for, once we've done our best to acquire them. If, for example, you know yourself to be most effective and comfortable as an Informational Leader, you might want to partner with a Charismatic Leader to make a presentation.

No one leadership style, to be sure, is the best or better than the rest. Each, as we've noted, has its strengths and weaknesses. The best leaders have at least some ability in all four styles. So it makes sense to know your strengths and weaknesses as a leader, build on your strong style(s), and increase your competence in the style(s) that are less comfortable. Leadership is a set of innate and acquired skill as well as a birthright. All the types can be both taught and learned. And as we just implied, collaborating with a leader of a different type, assuming the egos in question will allow it, can create a really strong leadership environment.

The Magical Relationship

There's magic in the relationship between leaders and followers that is dynamic as well as necessary for work to be effective and satisfying. The following story illustrates this point: *Marianne felt shy about stepping up to the requirements of her new leadership position. She just wanted to be liked by her staff by being "the same as everyone else." In her first months on the job, she never criticized anyone and kept herself in the background. Soon she was shocked when her department became chaotic and the employees began slumping. Her supervisor came to her assistance: "Marianne, to be a good leader, you must own and step into the responsibilities that go with your role. You must say 'yes' to the enhanced power you have. Equally important, your employees must say 'yes' to your leadership. That means they must be willing to trust you to be fair and clear. When both you and your employees say 'yes' to your leadership, then you will be able to work together in a productive and satisfying way—but not before."*

Cedar's most important learning about what she calls the "alchemy of yes" for leaders came from many years of working together with ten other friends presenting monthly spiritual-dance events. They were determined to explore shared leadership. After trying completely non-hierarchal leadership, they found that the events were most successful when one person functioned as what they called "the Weaver." This person was in charge. After the event, the team of ten debriefed and chose the next Weaver. This way everyone had chances to be both leader and follower. After being the leader, the ex-Weaver discovered how important being a good follower was to the success of the whole as well. As leaders, all ten learned to their amazement that when they said a full "yes" to leadership, they entered a larger "field" in which they were aware of group needs (like when to end the event, when to set clearer boundaries, when to open the space, when to speak, and when to be silent) than they had had as followers. Likewise they learned that if they gave a reluctant or perfunctory "yes" to leading, the followers wouldn't feel safe enough and couldn't fully participate.

Down-power Leadership

In our leadership explorations, we came to understand something we are now calling "down-power leadership." After being the Weaver for one event, Cedar was a follower whose task was to attend to the candles.

What a small thing! She thought. However, she found great pleasure and even meaning in doing this job impeccably. She made sure that not one of the dozens of candles placed around the room went out. At a philosophical level she felt as if she were holding the light so that all the participants would feel surrounded by it. In other words, she was saying a whole-hearted "yes" to her responsibility as a follower with a menial-seeming task. It wasn't her job to track activities or feelings in the larger field of the event. She was thus surprised by how meaningful her role felt and how satisfied and engaged she was in it. She also noticed some relief that she didn't have the larger responsibility of the Weaver's role and was glad that someone else she trusted was charged to do that. As followers, moreover, everyone learned that if they didn't say a full and clear "yes" to the Weaver, his or her leadership was compromised.

What is most important here is saying "yes" to both up- and down-power roles. The amount of power and the responsibilities of each may differ, but affirming one's participation in either role is the alchemy that moves people and projects along in a satisfying and effective way.

Saying "yes" in both up-and down-power roles has one additional complication. As you move closer to the ideal and magical relationship that we have described, the differences between these two roles can become blurred. You can experience yourself in what we would call a dual role of being friend and employer or friend and employee. This is okay and maybe even desirable, but the differences in roles still remain. As the up-power person, you may feel so attached to your friendship that you have difficulty making the assessments and decisions that go with your role responsibilities. As a down-power person, you may feel so attached to your friendship that you may find it difficult to accept assessments and decisions that have to be made in service of the larger vision.

Here are several other things to watch out for when you feel you are in a dual role having a relationship of simultaneous equality (friendship) and power differential.

- resentment or the feeling of being taken advantage of,
- wanting or attempting to take care of the other at your own expense,
- trying to be perfect,
- feeling abnormally guilty, wrong, or at fault,
- feeling surprised or confused by some behavior of the other,

- feeling confused about responsibilities that accompany each role, when and how to be in each role, and how to shift from one to another,
- feeling uncertain or burdened by having to share personal information, and/or
- discovering expectations based on the non-power-differential relationship that clash with the power-differential one.

When you notice any of these reactions, especially when you are in an up-power position, bring it or them to the other's attention so that you can creatively and effectively address and manage the feelings in question.

Here's a summary of the differences between up- and down-power roles and responsibilities.

UP-POWER	DOWN-POWER
Is 150% responsible.	Is $100% responsible.
Makes assessments.	Responds to assessments.
Is the ultimate decision-maker.	Responds to decisions.
Holds the bigger vision .	Holds a part of the total vision.
May hurt, exploit, or dominate.	Is at risk of hurt, exploitation, or domination.

When you are in a down-power role—and as you know, we all move back and forth or up and down in our personal, role, and status power—you have the opportunity for using your leadership power well in two ways.

1. **By accepting the scope and responsibilities of your down-power role.** This response means saying a full and energetic "yes" to your role, however limited. In this "yes" you can be strong, sincere, and effective. Your down-power leadership can be:

• *Informational*—You provide information to the up-power person in a complete, well-organized, and timely way.

• *Charismatic*—Your enthusiasm and energetic presence support and encourage your team and the up-power leader.

• *Relational*—You put energy into helping others stay connected and working well together to the extent that your down-power role allows.

• *Visionary*—You put meaning, creativity, and inspiration into whatever part you are responsible for.

Down-power leadership of this kind is mutually respectful and collaborative. Role boundaries are maintained, with tasks being carried out in the best possible way. This kind of down-power leadership is the ideal and certainly not true of all individual relationships, teams, or organizations all the time. However, it's a goal we can aspire to and achieve whenever we can.

2. **By working skillfully to help a person in an up-power role who is misusing power do better in this regard.** This kind of down-power leadership is quite challenging and complex. It requires maturity and skill and, to be honest, is sometimes not worth the risk. We want to talk about this possibility, though, since a negative attitude both disempowers and appears to condone the misuse of power. As described earlier, there are many reasons why people misuse power. Therefore, some leaders will be more open to down-power feedback and self-correction in the interest of collaboration than others. You can find suggestions in the "Resolve Difficulties" chapter and a longer list of tips in the "**Try This**" section of the book for effective ways to work with superiors who are misusing their power.

In both places you'll notice two kinds of suggestions. One focuses on creating a compassionate connection. For example: You can offer authentic appreciations, be willing to be part of the solution, avoid putting the superior on the spot, try to understand their point of view even if you don't agree with it, wait for a time when you are calm and not upset for a meeting, or put yourself in your superior's shoes as a means of feeling empathy. This is leadership of the heart—pure and simple.

The other is leadership of strength by selecting and using an appropriate strategy. Without losing compassion, you consider and employ tactics likely to get the results you want without your becoming a lightning rod or sacrificial lamb. For example, link a complaint with a request for change; be specific by describing the impact the superior's behavior has had on you or the system; find out where you have leverage that could have a positive effect; identify possible differences in communication or personality styles that may be interfering with good working relationships; feel when to persist and when to let go; and above all look for a win/win solution. Both compassion and strength are important for achieving what you want. By using both together in the proper proportions you will be able to stay in the Power Zone.

Here now is a chart that describes how up-power leaders can help those misusing their down-power role to own and use their power wisely and well. In other words, they can use their personal, role, status, and collective powers to move the other toward the right (literally) side of the chart.

The other set of arrows in the middle, meanwhile, describes how down-power leaders can help move up-power leaders to the right-use-of-power side of the diagram.

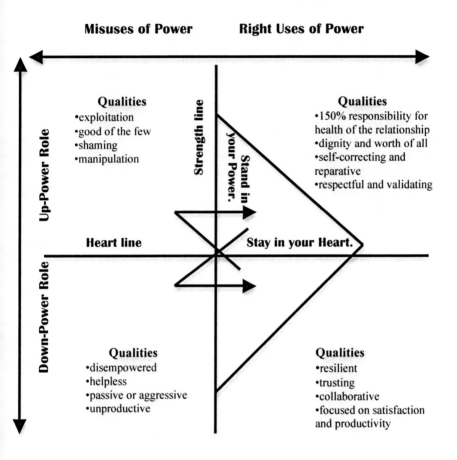

Misuses of Power   **Right Uses of Power**

Up-Power Role

Qualities
•exploitation
•good of the few
•shaming
•manipulation

Strength line

Stand in your Power.

Qualities
•150% responsibility for health of the relationship
•dignity and worth of all
•self-correcting and reparative
•respectful and validating

Heart line   **Stay in your Heart.**

Down-Power Role

Qualities
•disempowered
•helpless
•passive or aggressive
•unproductive

Qualities
•resilient
•trusting
•collaborative
•focused on satisfaction and productivity

Good leadership in both up- and down-power roles requires an integrated combination of heart and strength, compassion and strategy. At its highest and best, regardless of one's role, this combination is actually an alliance between compassionate and strategic interactions. The caring interactions lay a foundation of trust and intimacy which then supports the strategic interactions and the kind of taking charge needed to accomplish a task. Likewise, hierarchical responsibility and accountability in tandem create the foundation for the safety and freedom required for creative work. By using a dynamic balance between these two ways of expressing power, both up- or down-power individuals can help create a healthier work and relationship environment. Finding this balance is not easy, but through attention and good practices we can move relationships and systems toward right relatedness.

Here there be dragons.

We human beings are complex creatures. The ideal up-power/down-power relationship, like love and old age, is "not for sissies." Here's an interesting example of a situation in which neither party was using their power wisely and well.

Story: *Business consultants J.T. and Dale are responding to a question from a reader. J.T describes a man who felt his boss was threatened by him and was therefore singling him out for abusive treatment. J.T. then observed their interaction in a team meeting. "As the manager conducted the meeting, the other employees were nodding and smiling and making suggestions, but my client sat stoic, with arms folded and a scowl on his face. When the manager asked him for input, he simply said, 'Whatever you want,' at which point the manager became visibly agitated. After the meeting, the employee said, 'See! I agree with him, and he just gets mad!'" J.T. replied, "'I'd be mad at you too.' [J.T.] explained [that] he [the employee] was radiating disinterest and disrespect, despite his words." Dale suggested that instead of confronting the boss by telling the boss that he thinks he, the employee, feels threatened or continuing his disinterested and disrespectful behavior, he "ask the boss what he could do differently to gain his trust and encouragement." Then the employee could try following the suggestions and checking in with the boss in a couple of weeks to see how things were going. This approach could help the two toward becoming allies instead of remaining adversaries (J.T. O'Donnell and Dale Dauten, "Talk Jobs," *Denver Post, Feb. 3, 2013).

This story particularly interests us because it's an example of an interactional system in which both the boss and the employee are not using their power well. What doesn't the boss know in this situation? We're guessing he doesn't realize that as the up-power person he has 150% responsibility for the health of the working relationship. He also hasn't established a compassionate enough alliance so that this employee could settle into his down-power role. What doesn't the employee know? We speculate that he isn't aware of or sensitive to how his behavior in the meeting is impacting the boss. Nor does he seem able to imagine how his strategy of confrontation might impact his boss. In short, neither the boss nor the employee appears to have much understanding of the responsibilities, differences, and dynamics inherent in their differentiated power relationship. Here there be dragons, but there are also opportunities to improve the relationship from both side that would enable boss and employee to collaborate more effectively in future in their hierarchical workplace.

Story: *Nick's supervisor was unable to hear Nick's suggestions and observations. Instead, he shifted the blame to Nick for any issue that Nick brought up. Nick knew he was at great risk of being fired if he continued to speak his concerns. Others in his group had already decided to remain silent. Nick consulted with life coach and got help in strategizing. He convinced his other team members that they were at much less risk if they approached their supervisor together. Nick asked the supervisor for a meeting with the team and told him they had some concerns they'd like to talk with him about with the goal of an improved working environment. He also told the supervisor that they would prefer to work it out with him directly, but if he wasn't willing, they would take their concern up the chain of command if necessary. Nick's supervisor agreed to meet, and they worked the issue out. Nick skillfully used his compassion, his collective influence, his positive suggestions for change, and the hierarchy in this example of successful down-power leadership.*

The Emerging Power Paradigm

At the heart of living in the Power Zone is becoming part of the current paradigm shift to new and emerging uses of power, both personally and globally.

The old, but still dominant paradigm is the one in which getting and maintaining power is the main task, power as domination. You, we're sure, are very familiar with this system. It's based on ages-old Roman and then Machiavellian beliefs that in order to gain, sustain, and enhance power, one has to exploit and manipulate those power-down. Here are some of the rules, in their most recent form, from the book *The 48 Laws of Power* by Robert Greene (1998, 2000). *Law 3: Conceal your intentions. Law 4: Always say less than necessary. Law 11: Learn to keep people dependent on you. Law 12: Use selective honesty and generosity to disarm your victim. Law 15: Crush your enemy totally. Law 17: Keep others in suspended terror: Cultivate an air of unpredictability. Law 31: Control the options: Get others to play with the cards you deal.*

It's not very pleasant stuff, but it's certainly the model of power without heart, control without connection, and strategy without compassion. We mention it because it's important to acknowledge that this has been our dominant global understanding of power, and some lesser or more extreme versions of it are still in effect in many if not most organizations and nations. In the short run it gets things done. Think of how the Egyptian pyramids and the Cambodian temples in Siem Riep were built. The Domination System is motivated by overblown ego needs for wealth, control, fame, and immortality. In the long run, what is accomplished is outweighed by the egregious harm it causes human beings and the environment. As Gandhi put it, *"Object to violence because when it appears to do good, the good is only temporary; the evil it does is permanent."*

Wise observers in every culture have always understood the ultimate futility of the domination, or win/lose, model of power. Consider the famous short poem, "Ozymandias," by the English Romantic poet Percy Bysshe Shelley:

> I met a traveler from an antique land,
> Who said—"Two vast and trunkless legs of stone
> Stand in the desert. . . . Near them, on the sand,
> Half sunk a shattered visage lies, whose frown,
> And wrinkled lip, and sneer of cold command,
> Tell that its sculptor well those passions read
> Which yet survive, stamped on these lifeless things,
> The hand that mocked them, and the heart that fed;
> And on the pedestal, these words appear:
> 'My name is Ozymandias, King of Kings,
> Look on my Works, ye Mighty, and despair!'
>
> Nothing beside remains. Round the decay
> Of that colossal Wreck, boundless and bare
> The lone and level sands stretch far away."

The emerging paradigm that is slowly replacing the Domination System is what we might call the Empowerment System, which is a socially intelligent model. The Empowerment System is one in which the common good and the environment are high priorities in every endeavor. Both accomplishments *and* respectful relationships are seen as vital for success. As our friend Layne Longfellow puts it, "[It's] doing well by doing good." The new paradigm is Win/Win, not Win/Lose (which eventually, as in Ozymandias's case, turns out to be Lose/Lose).

Much more difficult to achieve than the Domination System, the Empowerment System requires skills and facilities on the part of up-power people in a whole range of healthy responses. The growth and effectiveness of this emerging paradigm also depends on the growth in wisdom and skill of those in down-power roles. The Empowerment System thrives when there is an alliance between up- and down-power persons. Both must come to understand the differences in responsibility that accompany their roles, especially in the case of up-power people the 150% Principle.

Internationally and politically, the Empowerment System resembles the skilled use of negotiation to resolve conflicts, financial support for health and welfare rather than arms, and an exponential rise in humanitarian non-governmental organizations. Joseph Nye calls these activities *soft power.* Hilary Clinton's term is *smart power.* Preston Nye (as quoted in Susan Cain's *Quiet,* p. 196) makes the comparison succinctly: *"Aggressive power beats you up; soft power wins you over."* Winning someone over creates an ally. Beating someone up creates an enemy. Much long-term healing and benefit can come from the determined, persistent, and skillful use of soft, or smart, power.

Gareth Evans in an article titled "The Global March Toward Peace" (Project Syndicate, December 29, 2012; first publicized by Andrew Mack's Human Security Project Report, www.hsrgroup.org) gives some statistics on the decline of violence as a response to conflict worldwide in the last 20 years. *"After a high point in the late 1980's and very early 1990's, there has been a decline of well over 50% in the number of major conflicts both between and within states; in the number of genocidal and other mass atrocities; and in the number of people killed as a result of them."*

As usual, findings like these get buried under media's focus on and fascination with violence. Apparently, bad news sells better than good. We were interested in Evans' explanations for this movement toward greater global peacefulness. He attributes it to *"the huge upsurge in conflict prevention, conflict management, negotiated peacemaking, and post-conflict peace-building activity that has occurred . . . most of it spearheaded by the much[-]maligned U.N.* For the duration of this greater peacefulness, he concludes that *"since the end of World War II, a fundamental normative shift has occurred among the major powers' policymakers. Having witnessed the ravages of the last century, they simply no longer see any virtue, nobility, or utility in waging war, and certainly not nuclear war."* Consequently, the world's governments are increasingly rejecting violence as a means to vanquish their enemies for an Empowerment System that considers peace the best and only viable option for building a sustainable future.

Marc Ian Barasch, whose study of compassion became the book *Field Notes on the Compassionate Life: A Search for the Soul of Kindness*, comments, *"[A] leading evolutionary biologist affirmed [that] 'Recent evidence [shows] directional trends in evolution [that] involve increases in empathy, affectionate attachment, and inter-subjective awareness.' Maybe, just maybe, after three and a half billion years of scrambling, clambering ascent, it's survival of the kindest from here on out."*

Soul Work and Ethical Wisdom

Changing our personal and collective expectations about right uses of power to one that embodies social intelligence and links power with heart is truly ethics-in-action. Yet we must build our inner capacity to use power with heart. That's where soul work comes in. We need to do whatever it takes to become kinder and gentler human beings, since, as the Indonesians of Java say, "Carpenters can't make tables better than themselves."

Movement toward better uses of power, however, also requires knowledge, motivation, discipline, and skill. We need to: 1) Learn to use our personal and professional power to prevent, reduce, or repair harm and promote well-being; 2) Campaign for a socially intelligent model of power; 3) Develop and use our skills to give and receive feedback; 4) Become ever more sensitive to our impact on others, especially those down-power from us; and 5) Strategically and skillfully cease to expect, condone, or feel helpless about misuses of power in systems and from power-up individuals. We must expect and demand social intelligence from ourselves and the others around us. This is the right use of soul power. It is also the heart of ethics.

This book invites you to soul work and growth in ethical wisdom. Linking soul work, power, and ethics together, Glenda Green says, *"Ethics is the ongoing process of applying principles of higher intelligence to the problems of personal and collective existence, and endowing life with values that support the well-being of all. Ethics is the care we show in affecting the lives of others as well as a sense for where one's greatest value lies in relation to others. Ethics might be summarized as cause and effect in balance, and applied for the greatest good."*

In the end, whether we take either the global or interpersonal view of living in the Power Zone, we can find much guidance from the treasury of the world's wisdom. Here is a small sampler.

God grant me the Serenity to accept the things I cannot change, the Courage to change the things I can, . . . the Wisdom to know the difference; and the Strength to try to change what should be changed even when the change cannot be immediately effected.
(Reinhold Niebuhr's Serenity Prayer, with additional words by Robbins Barstow)

At a time when we see so much evil, we are called upon to have the moral grandeur and spiritual audacity to believe in good, to proclaim it, to stand in conviction, to take the people who truly do evil and, yes, hold them accountable. But to nevertheless stand for the possibility of human redemption that turns even the hardest hearts.
(Marianne Williamson)

I just do the best I can and leave the rest to the greater soul.
(Bert Hellinger)

Do not let the fact that things are not made for you, that conditions are not as they should be, stop you. Go on anyway. Everything depends on those who go on anyway.
(Robert Henri from *The Art Spirit*)

We are not here to save the world. We are here to love and serve the world, and in that love and in that service, the world may or may not be changed.
(Gurumail)

Conclusion

RIGHT USE OF POWER

CONCLUSION:

Check the Contents of Your Power Toolbox

When Reynold Ruslan was a university dean, he was asked by his president to co-lead the effort to revise the institution's general-education requirements. He began by asking his committee to consider this question: "What should every college graduate, regardless of major, know and be able to do on graduation?" What, in short, were the essential skills and abilities that an educated person in the late 20th Century (as it was then) needed to possess and be able to use for a successful, meaningful life?

In this spirit, we'd like to list out the Power-Tools (PTs) and Power Concepts (PCs) we think you should have at the ready in your Toolbox for Living. Unsurprisingly, these are the very concepts and techniques we have discussed in the preceding chapters. We'll use the "Pi" symbol (for Power) in lieu of bullets as we list them. For easy reference, we have divided the items by chapter so you can go back and review them whenever you like. Note that the earlier chapters are dominated by Power Concepts, since we needed to build a framework of ideas before introducing our Power Tools. Finally, Power Tools are set off from the Power Concepts by being written in **bold letters**.

Here goes.

Chapter One

Π   (PC) Power is the ability to have an effect or to have influence.

Π   (PC) Power is relational—it takes place in the give-and-take of interpersonal relations.

Π   (PC) Power is our human birthright; we all have it to a greater or lesser extent.

Π   (PC) Ethical behavior consists of using our power wisely and well.

Π   (PC) The right use of power includes (1) preventing, resolving, and repairing harm, (2) improving relationships and situations, (3) balancing strength with heart, and (4) promoting well-being and serving the common good.

Π   (PC) Using power well requires more than good intentions.

Π   (PC) Power is value-neutral. The way power is used gives it a positive or negative value.

Π   (PC) The four kinds of power are (1) personal, (2) role, (3) status, and (4) collective.

Π   (PC) Personal power is our in-born power as an individual. Everyone has at least some.

Π   (PC) Role power is power that comes with a role or position; it is ascribed power.

Π   (PC) Power roles shift. A mail clerk at work will be more powerful as a parent at home.

Π   (PC) In any interpersonal relation, one party is up-power while the other is down-power.

Π   (PC) Status power is culturally determined, e.g., Asian elders have more status power than Western ones, while Western women have more status power than Arab women.

Chapter Two

Π   (PC) The Power Differential consists of the perceived power differences between up- and down-power parties in any relationship.

Π   (PC) Down-power doesn't mean being powerless, and up-power doesn't mean having unlimited power.

Π   (PC) Down-power people are more vulnerable and at risk than up-power ones.

Π   (PC) Contrarily, the words and deeds of up-power individuals have more influence, for better or worse, than those of their down-power associates. Unnderstanding these dynamics is vital in up-power roles.

Π (PC) Up-power people thus have more responsibility than down-power ones in any power-differential relationship.

Π (PT) **Consequently, whenever we are the up-power party in such a relationship, we apply the 150% Principle, whereby both parties are 100% responsible for the health of the relationship, but the up-power party, by being more powerful, is even more responsible. Arbitrarily we say that their responsibility is 50% greater.**

Chapter Three

Π (PC) To use our power well, we need to be sensitive and aware.

Π (PT) *Curiosity* **is an excellent Power Tool, since it helps us find what we need to know to prevent or repair harm in any interpersonal situation.**

Π (PT) *The Golden Thread,* **or the positive learning available from all (especially negative) experiences, can help us improve our future uses of power. So the Power Tool is to seek the Golden Thread in every situation and then apply it.**

Π (PT) *Maintaining Healthy Boundaries,* **whether up- or down-power, helps prevent harm in interpersonal encounters.**

Π (PT) *Remaining Moderate and Flexible in Our Boundaries* **is essential to staying in the Power Zone: neither over- nor under-bounded, controlling nor easily controlled.**

Π (PC) In interactions our intentions do not always correspond with our impacts.

Π (PT) **We must thus be sensitive and** *track* **how our words or actions actually impact others, since it's the impact not the intention that counts.**

Chapter Four

Π (PC) Power with Heart enlivens ourselves and others, while Power without Heart is ultimately destructive of self, others, and our relationships.

Π   **(PT) Living in the Power Zone requires that we apply Right-Use-of-Power Concepts and Tools to *All Sentient Beings and the Earth Itself*, not just other persons.**

Π   (PC) Like it or not, we are all role models to others.

Π   **(PT) Strive to use Right-Use-of-Power Concepts and Tools *always* and *everywhere* since others are almost always watching and will often copy what we do.**

Π   **(PT) Living in the Power Zone means *Staying Vigilantly Between* the *Extremes* of being directive & responsive, firm & flexible, task-focused & relationship-focused, strength-centered & heart-centered, over-powering & under-powering, and extroverted & introverted. Finding just the right place in each situation is the goal.**

Π   **(PT) Requesting, giving, receiving, and using *Feedback* skillfully and appropriately are together a major Power Tool.**

Π   **(PT) *Kindness* and *Appreciation* are among the most effective forms of feedback.**

Chapter Five

Π   (PC) Empowering ourselves—"strengthening our core"—is a requirement for living in the Power Zone.

Π   (PC) The opposite, inadequate self-care, may lead us to misuse our power.

Π   **(PT) *Good Self-care* consists of (1) an *Appropriate Work-load*, (2) a *Diversified Life*, including play, (3) *Service*, and (4) *Moderation*.**

Π   **(PT) Developing *Resilience*—the ability to bounce back—is an essential Power Tool.**

Π   **(PT) *Use Technology Carefully*, without becoming an addict.**

Π   (PC) When we are not empowered, we can't empower others.

Chapter Six

Π (PC) The earlier we detect the harm we may be causing, the easier it is to effect a resolution.

Π **(PT)** *Compassion, Curiosity,* **and** *Non-defensiveness* **are the best tools to begin resolving conflicts.**

Π **(PT) First, though, take** *Three Deep Breaths.*

Π **(PT)** *Gaining Compassion* **for someone we've hurt can be achieved by recalling a time when someone hurt us.**

Π **(PT)** *Good Tracking* **can lead to early detection of harm that has been caused.**

Π **(PT) Some or all of these** *Five Steps* **can repair harm we've caused as an up-power person:** **(1)** *Acknowledging* **our misused power, (2)** *Explaining* **our intention, (3)** *Expressing* **regret, (4)** *Admitting* **we've learned from our mistake, and (5)** *Helping* **re-start the relationship.**

Π (PC) Repairing harm from a down-power position is trickier and riskier than from an up-power one.

Π **(PT) To do so we should (1)** *Reflect* **on what occurred, (2)** *Learn* **what we can, (3)** *Strategize,* **(4)** *Implement* **our plan, (5)** *Forgive,* **and (6)** *Let Go* **and** *Move On.*

Chapter Seven

Π (PC) Why people misuse power and act unethically is ultimately a mystery.

Π (PC) Reasons range from naïveté and ignorance through insensitivity, lack of skill, poor judgment, and shame to just plain malice.

Π (PC) There seems to be cross-cultural agreement on the importance to society of honesty, responsibility, respect, and fairness.

Π (PC) Empathy and altruism, moreover, seem hard-wired in us human beings through our so-called "social engagement" nervous system.

П (PC) Shame is one of the biggest barriers to using our power well *and* resolving conflicts.

П **(PT)** *Physical Techniques* **like moving, stretching, humming, smiling, and laughing can** *Free Us* **from the** *Shame Dungeon.*

П (PC) The Power Paradox means that the more power people get, the more difficult it is for them to use it well.

П **(PT)** *Awareness* **of the Power Paradox and development of a** *Good Character* **can** *Keep Us from* **over-identifying with our worldly success and** *Misusing our Power.*

Chapter Eight

П (PC) Using power well is the primary task of a leader.

П (PC) The four kinds of leader, whether up- or down-power, are (1) Information-based, (2) Charismatic, (3) Relational, and (4) Visionary.

П (PC) The best leaders, despite tending to be strongest in one or two of these areas, generally have or attempt to develop strength in all four.

П **(PT) We must** *Analyze Our Strengths and Weaknesses as Leaders* **and** *Work for Continuous Improvement.*

П **(PT) For leaders to success,** *both Leaders and* **their** *Followers* **must "say yes" to their leadership role. (We call this phenomenon the "Alchemy of Yes.")**

П (PC) Down-power people can also lead, but they must be skillful and strategic in doing so.

П **(PT) Sometimes** *Down-power People need to Ally with their Peers* **to succeed** *in Correcting an Up-power Person* **who has misused power.**

П (PC) Good leadership both up-power and down requires that the individual balance strength with heart, or intelligence with compassion.

П (PC) Sooner or later misusers of power if uncorrected or unrepentant will get their due, but often not before damage, sometimes great damage, has been done. (Think of Hitler.)

Π (PC) The Right Use of Power needs to be cultivated at both the individual and social levels for the world to become a better place for all of us and our descendants.

Π **(PT)** *Working on Ourselves* **and our** *Institutions* **to learn** *To Use Power Better* **is without doubt** *the Way Forward to* **achieving a** *Better World.*

Concluding Word

So what can YOU do? Here are some suggestions.

1. Put the concepts and techniques found here into practice. Use this book as a workbook.

2. Create Right Use of Power Teams with your friends and neighbors. Then work through this program together. It's often more fun that way than on your own.

3. Use our website (www.rightuseofpower.com) to find additional products and resources, many without cost, to further your study.

4. Subscribe at our website to our free monthly Right Use of Power Newsletter.

5. Attend a Right Use of Power workshop scheduled near you. Check our website—www.rightuseofpower.com—for the continuously updated Workshop Schedule.

6. Coordinate a Right Use of Power workshop in your area. We are always looking for new workshop coordinators, and we will pay you for your efforts. We have a growing international guild of Right Use of Facilitators—some generalists and some specializing in areas like business, education, parenting, government, the justice system, etc.—who would be delighted to lead a workshop in your area.

7. Consider translating this book into one of the world's languages—something you can do as a volunteer (We are a nonprofit organization, after all.)—or for pay. (We would explore getting a grant to underwrite your translation services.)

8. Attend a special workshop after the regular one to become trained as a Right Use of Power workshop facilitator.

9. Think about become part of our sales team for this book. Since we are self-publishing *Living in the Power Zone* and want to get our message out as widely as possible, we are working with our facilitators and other friends in a profit-sharing arrangement: one-third to the Institute, one-third to our sales associates, and one third to us as authors.

10. Friend and/or Like us on Facebook or follow us on Twitter.

11. Contact us with your feedback—ideas, suggestions for improvement of this book or our website, whatever comes to mind. You can reach us at info@rightuseofpower.com. The two of us believe that the wisdom of the many almost always trumps the wisdom of the few. Isn't that the basic idea behind democracy—especially in light of the saying "God don't make no junk"?

Finally, thank you for reading this book. We apologize for anything that didn't make sense or struck you as inappropriate. We did our level best to share helpful ideas and practices clearly and concisely. Since we'll be regularly updating this book and soon publishing it as an e-book on Amazon.com as well, we intend to improve and refine it over time. That's why your feedback is so important. Indeed, the ability to making ongoing improvements is one of the main reasons for our using publication on demand, the major way to self-publish.

We hope your reading has repaid you with some new ideas and a few useful techniques you can apply to your life. Above all, we hope you'll commit right here, right now to try your best to live your life in the Power Zone, a place where you will be using your personal, role, status, and collective power for your own good and that of everyone else. For all your attempts to use your power wisely and well, we wish you success and Godspeed.

Sincerely,

Cedar Barstow & Reynold Ruslan Feldman

APPENDIX:

Try This!

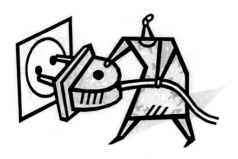

TRY THIS #1 (Ch. 3): Remember a Time

This is a self-reflective process described as a story in Chapter 3, the purpose of which is to help you explore your history in relation to up-power persons. Try this process with a friend. We've all been hurt by misuses or abuses of power, some of us more deeply than others. Turning your awareness inside, ask your unconscious to offer you a memory of a time you were hurt by someone in authority. It shouldn't be a strongly traumatic memory but one you could still learn and heal from. Now notice where you are, who you are with, how old you are, what you are wearing, the time of year, and other details. Then, without putting in a lot of effort, ask yourself these things.

1. What happened?	2. What was the impact on this relationship?
3. What would you have needed from the person who hurt you (that you didn't get) that would have made things turn out okay?	4. What decisions about power did you make as a result of this event?
How else has this experience impacted you?	What did the person who hurt you NOT know?
What did you learn from this experience ("your golden thread")?	Have you over-compensated in any way as a result of this experience? How?

Now, return to your normal consciousness and reflect a bit on your experience. You could use thought, writing, or drawing as a medium.

TRY THIS #2 (Ch. 2): Cultural Beliefs and Messages

To explore how your use of power has been affected by cultural messages and conditioning, try filling in this form for one or more of these cultural categories. You may wish to use separate sheets of paper.

CULTURE	MESSAGE
• Class • Sex • Ethnicity • Race • Age • Education • Employment • Sexual Orientation • Religious Preference • Physical or Mental Disabilities	A. MESSAGE received about power. B. HOW does the message affect how I use my personal and/or role power? C. Have these messages caused me to feel DISEMPOWERED? D. What are some NEW WAYS OF THINKING, FEELING, OR BEHAVING that might help me moderate the impact of these beliefs and make me feel more powerful?
	A.
	B.
	C.
	D.

TRY THIS #3 (Ch. 4): Power Parameters

Here are a few experiments for stretching what's comfortable for you as you practice living in the Power Zone. The healthy range is indicated by the gray-toned area. The healthy zone for each parameter is thus toward the middle, somewhat away from either extreme. Power without some heart and heart without some strength will take you out of the zone on any parameter. The strength side is on the left; the heart side on the right.

First, using a colored marker, put a dot on each continuum to indicate the place where you tend to be. This would be your most natural, habitual, and comfortable place—or your default spot.

Then, using different colors, compare this spot to other contexts, like where would you place yourself in intimate relationships, at work, or as a child. Add other contexts of your own. What do you discover about yourself? Next, imagine yourself at each extreme and observe how abuses of power happen there. At the extremes, we lose heart, and thus our care and connection with each other. Notice how much more range you have now than when you were a child. What positive things become possible when you expand your range a bit with any parameter? Try this learning game in a room with some friends. Set up each continuum going from one wall to another. Place yourselves physically along the continuum. Then walk to a less comfortable location. After, discuss the experience among yourselves.

	extroverted	_____	introverted	
	directive	_____	responsive	
	firmly boundaried	_____	flexibly boundaried	
	task focused	_____	relationship focused	
	persistent	_____	letting go	
	truth focused	_____	harmony focused	
	strength centered	_____	heart centered	
	over-powering	_____	under-powering	
	extroverted	_____	introverted	

TRY THIS #4 (Ch. 4): Smoothing the Way

Here's another process to try when you are stuck. It can help you move from Reactive to Pro-Active.

Try some or all of these five elements.	
The action:	Say what happened. Use no emotive words.
Your response:	How you feel or how it affected you. No blame. You may want to explain why you feel that way.
Preferred outcome:	What you'd like to be able to do or have, or simply: "I'd like to work something out together." No demands. Make it an invitation.
Constructive consequence:	Describe the benefit(s) of the outcome you are suggesting.
Invitation to respond:	Encourage a conversation.

Here's an example: In this case, your manager is not giving you feedback. *"When I don't get the information on how I am doing on the project, I feel unsure about how it's going. I'd like some feedback so that I could know if it is proceeding well or if there are adjustments I need to make."*

Practice: Think of a personal or work situation that has been (or seems) difficult. Try using the formula, above. Write your answers in the spaces below or on a separate sheet.

When _____

I _____

What I'd like is _____

That way _____

Invite a response: _____

TRY THIS #5 (Ch. 4): Appreciation Circle*

At an appropriate time during a meeting, invite people to express appreciation for each other in this form. One person chooses another member of the group and then, using the person's name, completes this statement: "Jim, I appreciate you for _____." Jim then chooses someone else to appreciate. Each person chooses someone who has not yet been chosen to appreciate until the web is completed by the last person, who appreciates the person who began the circle.

Results include strengthened connections, increased warmth, and more individual self-confidence.

A few notes about appreciation and acknowledgement.

- Be alert not to overuse praise with the result that it loses value.
- Use praise only when you really mean it. Your praise must remain trustworthy.
- Try to give praise right away. Praise offered immediately has greater impact.
- Be as specific and accurate as you can.
- "Name the act, not the actor."
- Remember that we all long for appreciation.

After, discuss with each other what the impact of this activity was for you.

This exercise was taken from Cornelius and Faire, Everyone Can Win, *pp. 89-90, Used with permission.*

TRY THIS # 6: (Chs. 6 & 8): Tips for Handling Difficult Superiors

1. Offer authentic appreciations.
2. Link a complaint with a request for change.
3. Ask for a good time to talk.
4. Avoid taking something on alone when there is significant risk—join with others for solidarity and effectiveness.
5. Be specific and describe the (negative) impact of the superior's behavior on you and/or the system.
6. Use simplicity, consistency, and persistency.
7. Name possible solutions and be willing to be part of the solution.
8. Be clear about what outcome you want; then don't be attached to this particular outcome.
9. Try not to put the superior on the spot.
10. Try to understand his or her position even if you don't agree with it.
11. Focus more on how you want things to be in the future and less on the past.
12. Identify possible differences in leadership or communication style that may be causing conflict.
13. Find out where you have positive leverage and use it.
14. Stand in your strength and stay in your heart. Be forceful but also compassionate.
15. Ask your superior for feedback and respond to it.
16. When you CAN'T do what you want to do, identify what you CAN do.
17. Change a gripe into a curiosity about what might be possible.
18. Ask for a response by saying something like, "I need to know that you've heard me."
19. Learn when to persist and when to let go.
20. Try to have the largest possible perspective on the situation.
21. Enlist your superior in advocating for something or someone.
22. Plant seeds of change and then water them.
23. Be clear and direct, calm and authentic.
24. Describe the likely impacts of various alternative solutions.
25. Understand when you are triggered; then wait for a time when you are calmer.
26. "If you want a kitten, start by asking for a horse," i.e., use bargaining strategy.
27. Look for a WIN/WIN solution.
28. Use humor.

TRY THIS #7 (Ch. 6): Releasing the Past

When you feel haunted by an unresolved misuse or abuse of power, try this process to help you release it. It is based on Cedar's model for ethical decision-making called the Power Spiral. In this model there are four dimensions of right use of power to consider: Information/Presence, Compassion/Awareness, Connectedness/Accountability, and Skillfulness/ Wisdom. See the model on page 175. The purpose is to discern what action(s) right now would be the best use of your power and influence.

In the Information and Presence dimension:
- Why is this issue re-surfacing now?
- What is your present understanding of what happened to both you and the other(s)? Are there other sources of relevant information?
- Are there organizational guidelines or an ethics code that would be appropriate or useful to consult?

In the Compassion and Awareness dimension:
- What specifically do you feel sad and upset about?
- What might block resolving or repairing this conflict?
- With compassion for all concerned, what does your heart say?

In the Connectedness and Accountability dimension:
- Can you contact the person who caused the harm?
- What would you need to repair the situation?
- What actions feel right? Are you willing to take them?

In the Skillfulness and Wisdom dimension:
- How can you skillfully perform the actions you can take?
- What resources for support are available to you?
- How and when will you let go of the situation?

You may do this process alone but better would be to invite a friend or colleague to be present with you (Releasing the Past, p. 2).

- On a table or the floor, place a brief statement of the situation you want to resolve.

Releasing the Past, page 2

•Then place four pieces of paper with one of these words on each: INFORMATION, COMPASSION, CONNECTEDNESS, and SKILLFULNESS in four directions around the problem statement in the center.

•Now imagine you have special glasses that help you see through the perspective of each dimension as you respond to the questions, above, for each.

• Let yourself take in what each dimension offers you, especially surprises, new feelings, or new possibilities.

• You might literally move to each direction as you ask "its" questions so you can more easily embody each perspective.

•When you have completed this reflective process, take a moment to become quiet to see if anything else comes to you.

Here is an example of what the process yielded for one of our students:

> • *From the Information perspective she understood that, although there was an organizational ethics code, the misuse of power was a potent but subtle one that wasn't specifically listed in the code. She also saw how old this event was and that there wasn't actually much value in bringing it back to the organization. "Too much water over the dam," she said.*
> • *From the Compassion perspective she felt how deeply "stuck" she was in the hurt and that it was she, herself, who might get in the way of healing because of being somehow attached to the pain. She also found, to her surprise, that she could feel how she was already beginning to forgive.*
> • *From the Connectedness dimension she didn't know if the person who wounded her was available for contact, but she felt it was worth giving it a try. She decided to contact her with the overall goal of initiating some healing. What she wanted was an acknowledgement of her feelings, an understanding of what the other's intentions were, an apology, and a sense of completion.*
> • *From the Skillfulness dimension she decided that the wisest way to proceed would be to send an email asking if he would be available to talk or email about a painful situation from the past that she would like to understand more about and feel done with. If the person responded positively, she would re-connect with heart and strength, keeping in mind that her goal was healing and letting go, not blame or punishment. If this person was not available or did not respond, she would sit down with a friend and create a letting- go process.*

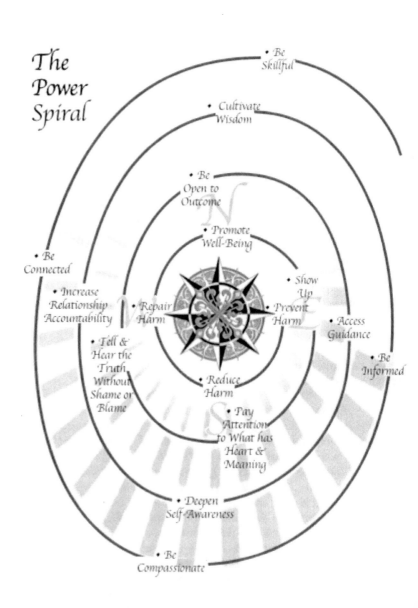

The
Power
Spiral

• Be Skillful

• Cultivate Wisdom

• Be Open to Outcome

• Promote Well-Being

• Be Connected

• Show Up

• Increase Relationship Accountability

• Repair Harm

• Prevent Harm

• Access Guidance

• Tell & Hear the Truth Without Shame or Blame

• Reduce Harm

• Be Informed

• Pay Attention to What has Heart & Meaning

• Deepen Self-Awareness

• Be Compassionate

TRY THIS #8 (Ch. 7): De-Activating Shame

When you, a friend, or colleague are stuck in the Shame Dungeon, this diagram can help you get out of it.

Shame Dungeon

**to de-activate shame   *(time)*   to de-activate shame
for the one harmed   for the one causing harm**

What's needed:

• Simple movements of arms and legs, rotating head to re-orient,
activating senses, breathing in, humming, speaking, touching, making eye contact
• Connection with a compassionate, non-judgmental listener

• Reality check

• Safe place to express anger, blame, resentment, and betrayal	• Safe place to express remorse, guilt, regret, and sorrow
• Opportunity to grieve and heal	• Opportunity to deal successfully with the underlying issues.
• Restored self-respect and empowerment	• Restored self-respect and self-worth
• Regained ability to be connected	• Regained ability to be connected
• Openness to receive reparation and/or apology and to be forgiving	• Openness to self-correction, giving reparation, and being forgiven
• Willingness to let go, heal, and move on	• Willingness to heal, grow, and move on

**Re-connection
with self, others,
and reality**

TRY THIS #9 (Ch. 8): Leadership Skills

Consciousness, empathy, and skillfulness are needed in both power-differential roles. Here are a few dynamics to be conscious of when using your power in either role. Check the ones that currently apply.

Up-Power Skills and Attitudes

_____1. I usually take ownership of my power role.

_____2. I usually keep appropriate role boundaries and limits.

_____3. I can usually stay in my heart while standing in my heart.

_____4. I am usually self-aware and able to self-correct.

_____5. I usually listen and respond well even to negative feedback.

_____6. I am usually able to address and resolve conflict.

_____7. I am usually in good contact with my client or group.

_____8. I practice being flexible in my responses in the power zone.

_____9. I usually practice the 150% Principle.

_____10. I usually honor and work well with differences.

Down-Power Skills and Attitudes

_____1. I usually feel strong and good in my role.

_____2. I rarely delay by too much questioning and/or doubting.

_____3. I am usually self-aware and able to self-correct.

_____4. I usually work efficiently and productively.

_____5. I am usually as collaborative as the situation requires.

_____6. When I have a complaint, I usually link it with a suggestion for change.

_____7. I understand the dynamics of the power differential.

_____8. I usually follow through with my agreements.

_____9. I am usually present and available.

_____10. I practice being flexible in my responses in the power zone.

To increase your skillfulness, pick one or several of these behaviors to improve.

TRY THIS #10: The Power Staff

During Right Use of Power Workshops, participants make "power staffs" using sticks or stones or any other object they would like to become a representation of how they want to be in relationship with their power in the future. We think you might like to make one too. People all over the world now have these power objects in their homes.

Story: The idea for making power objects came from an eventful ceremony that Cedar attended in a Native American kiva in Southern Colorado in the 1980's. The ceremony was skillfully led by Elizabeth Cogburn. As Cedar tells it, the participants, dancing ceremonially to drums, rattles, and voices throughout the night, gradually entered an altered state. The instructions were to "dance with whatever came up" for each person—staying aware and connected rather than falling asleep. Cedar found herself face to face with an image, memory, or dream of a native chief who protected his people well but did so with extreme violence. She was appalled to find that she could have the capacity for feeling such violence inside herself. She was at the time a shy, timid person who avoided leadership because she felt that course was the best way to do no harm. She wanted to go to sleep and get away from this image and what it seemed to mean. But she nonetheless danced with the image until she became curious about this warrior. She discovered two things that surprised her: he was very lonely, and he was totally devoted to his people. His love, however, was causing great harm to other tribal groups. After many hours, he and Cedar came to an agreement that he would teach her how to own and use her power, and she would teach him how to use his without violence. At the following morning's give-away circle, she received a staff with the guidance to let the stick talk to her and tell her how it wanted to be embellished." Over the next year her power staff emerged, and she began using it ceremonially. She claimed her power and soon understood it as a tool to be skillfully and wisely used to promote well-being and the common good.

Here's how to make a power staff of your own. You can do this alone or with a group of friends or colleagues. Gather interesting art supplies like string, glue, scissors, beads, shells, feathers, items of special personal meaning, and a stick of any size to make into a staff. (Or use a stone or other natural object.) Lay this collection of art supplies out on a sheet in the middle of the room and allow time (at least an hour) to create. Begin with a centering meditation to focus attention on the qualities and feelings you want to bring forth in the staff. To close, reflect privately or talk among yourselves about your power staffs; share stories, meanings, insights, and/or intentions. You might each want to stand holding your staff and claim your power with a strong and heart-felt "yes."

TRY THIS #11: Power Circles

This process, for groups of three to ten, can be done as part of a weekly group or in one or a few sessions. Over time, members can experience much depth, learning, and support. The purpose is to help people integrate what they are learning about their power and how to use it wisely by increasing their sense of empowerment, sharing feelings, listening to and learning from each other.

Go around to each participant one question at a time. Listen to each other with interest and compassion. Note that the process works best if people don't interrupt or comment. *(Thanks to Sarah Hartzel for her version of this exercise, which uses the phrase "I am a peacemaker.")*

1. First round: **I felt powerful** (or empowered*)* **this week when**

_____.
This is a time for remembering that you know what being empowered feels like. Your short response can come from work, home, the community. or the world,
   • Complete your turn by saying: **I am powerful.** Others repeat,
   Yes,_____ *(your name)***, you are powerful.**
   (This is a verbal affirmation for yourself.)

2. Second round: *(Note: This statement is made at the second* session. **Something related to my commitment from last week is**

_____
This response gives you a chance to reflect on the results of your commitment from the previous round.
   • Complete your turn by saying: **I am powerful.** Others repeat,
   Yes,_____ *(your name)***, you are powerful**

3. Third round: **A situation that is challenging (or an opportunity)** **for using my power wisely and well is** _____.
   Using my power wisely and well in this situation would look like

_____.
   • Complete your turn by saying: **I am powerful.** Others repeat,
   Yes,_____ *(your name)***, you are powerful.**

4. Fourth round: **In the name of empowerment, this week I will**

_____.
(This action should be something specific, doable, and measurable.)
   • Complete your turn by saying: **I am powerful.** Others repeat,
   Yes,_____ *(your name)***, you are powerful.**

TRY THIS #12~Power in the Movies

Choose a movie with some interesting examples of right or wrong uses of power. Gather a group, show it, and then discuss the power dynamics in it. Here are some good films to start with:

Lincoln (2012)

David Brooks describes the complexities of this movie and of Lincoln and his politics in "Why We Love Politics," The New York Times, Nov. 22, 2012. Brooks says, *"The challenge of politics lies precisely in the marriage of high vision and low cunning. . . . The movie . . .illustrates . . . that politics is the best place to develop the highest virtues. Politics involves such a perilous stream of character tests: how low can you stoop to conquer without destroying yourself; when should you break from it; how do you wrestle with the temptations of fame—that the people who can practice it and remain intact, like Lincoln, Washington, or Churchill, are incredibly impressive."*

Brooks continues, *"[There is another] step in the character-building trajectory, what you might call the loneliness of command. Toward the end of the Civil War, Lincoln had to choose between two rival goods, immediate peace and the definitive end of slavery. He had to scuttle a peace process that would have saved thousands of lives in order to achieve a larger objective."*

What do you think about these issues? We think they apply in most leadership positions, not just politics.

Beyond Right and Wrong (2012)

www.beyondrightandwrongthemovie.org) *1 hour 30 minutes*
This film is about the courage and depth of heart and soul that forgiveness requires, and the freedom and transformation that it brings. Extraordinary stories of reconciliation and acceptance from Rwanda, Northern Ireland, and Israel/ Palestine compel appreciation and shared heartache. The filmmaker says that through making this film, she came to understand that given certain extreme circumstances, all of us are capable of doing almost anything.

Issues that arise in this movie include: how are we taught to kill, what it actually takes to forgive even a murderer, what the stages of moving toward forgiveness are, what forgiveness makes possible, and what happens when we continue to think of the other party as evil.

Here are four more: *Les Miserables, Lars and the Real Girl, It's a Wonderful Life,* and *Oz the Great and the Powerful.* Let us know some others to add to our list. Email us at info@rightuseofpower.com. Thanks.

Many Realms Publishing
1485 Sumac Ave.
Boulder, CO 80304
Cell: 720-480-1342

Other Books by Cedar Barstow

Chapter 16, Earth Song, The Nature and Function of Rituals: Fire from Heaven, Edited by Ruth-Inge Heinze, Bergin & Garvey: 2000.

Right Use of Power: Ethics for the Helping Professions, Many Realms Publishing: 2002 (A complete manual for teaching the Right Use of Power ethics approach).

Seeds: A Collection of Art by Women Friends, Many Realms Publishing: 1976.

Tending Body and Spirit: Massage and Counseling with Elders, Many Realms Publishing: 1985.

Other Books by Reynold Ruslan Feldman

A World Treasury of Folk Wisdom, with Cynthia A. Voelke, HaroerCollins: 1992.

Stories I Remember—My Pilgrimage to Wisdom: A Spiritual Autobiography, Wisdom Foundation Publishing: 2009.

Wisdom—Daily Reflections for a New Era, Saint Mary's Press, 2000.

Wising Up—A Youth Guide to Good Living, with M. Jan Rumi, Cowley Publications: 2007.

Related Reading

Barasch, Marc Ian, *Field Notes on the Compassionate Life: A Search for the Soul of Kindness*, Rodale: 2005.

Beck, Don, and Cowan, Christopher, *Spiral Dynamics: Mastering Values, Leadership, and Change*, Blackwell Publishing: 1996.

Brooke, Melody, *Cycles of the Heart: A Way out of the Egocentrism of Everyday Life*, www.melodybrooke.com: 2006.

Cain, Susan, *Quiet: The Power of Introverts in a World that Can't Stop Talking*, Crown Publishers, New York: 2012.

Cornelius, Helena, and Faire, Shoshana, *Everyone Can Win: Responding to Conflict Constructively*, Simon and Schuster, Australia: 2006.

Fisher, Roger; Ury, William, and Patton, Bruce, *Getting to Yes*, Penguin Books: 1983.

Fuller, Robert, *Somebodies and Nobodies: Overcoming the Abuse of Rank*, New Society Publishers: 2003.

Gerzon, Mark, *Leading Beyond Borders: Thinking Globally and Acting Locally for a Just, Sustainable World*, www.mediatorsfoundation.org: 2004.

Hawkins, David, *Power Vs. Force: The Hidden Determinants of Human Behavior*, Hay House: 2002.

Karen, Robert, *Shame*, The Atlantic Monthly, February 1992.

Kurtz, Ron, *Body-Centered Psychotherapy, The Hakomi Method*, Life Rhythm: 1990.

Kidder, Rushworth, *Shared Values for a Troubled World: Conversations with Men and Women of Conscience*, Jossey-Bass: 1994.

Lakoff, George, *Don't Think of an Elephant*, Chelsea Green: 2004.

Popov, Linda Kavelin, *The Family Virtues Guide, Simple Ways to Bring Out the Best in Our Children and Ourselves,* Plume: 1997.

Rosenberg, Marshall, *Nonviolent Communication: A Language of Life*, Puddle Dancer Press: 2003.

Senge, Peter, Scharmer, C. Otto, Jaworski, Joseph, and Flowers, Betty Sue, *Presence—An Exploration of Profound Change in People, Organizations, and Society*, Currency Doubleday: 2004.

Stone, Douglas, Patton, Bruce, and Heen, Sheila, *Difficult Conversations: How to Discuss What Matters Most*, Penguin Books: 1999.

Ury, William, *The Third Side,* Penguin Books: 1999.

Watkins, Jane Magruder, and Mohr, Bernard, *Appreciative Inquiry: Change at the Speed of Imagination,* Jossey-Bass: 2001.

Wheatley, Margaret, and Kellner-Rogers, Myron, *A Simpler Way,* Berrett-Koehler Publishers, Inc.: 1996.

Chapman, Troy K., *Stepping Up: Wholeness Ethics for Prisoners and Those Who Care About Them,* The Whole Way Press: 2011.

CPSIA information can be obtained
at www.ICGtesting.com
Printed in the USA
FFOW05n1027050414

9 780974 374635